xkcd

xkcd
volume 0

Randall Munroe

breadpig
SAN FRANCISCO • THE INTERNETS

Printed in the United States of America

For information about special discounts for bulk purchases,
please contact Breadpig, Inc. at IncredibleBulk@Breadpig.com

Manufacturing by RR Donnelley

Munroe, Randall.
xkcd.
ISBN 978-0-615-31446-4
Breadpig, Inc.
www.breadpig.com

Breadpig is not a traditional publisher. The majority of the profits of this book are going to the artist, Randall Munroe. And as with all breadpig projects, the company's profits are being donated to a worthy charity. We selected the organization Room to Read (*RoomToRead.org*) which builds schools, establishes libraries, and promotes child education throughout the developing world. If you're one of those students reading this in your new school, we're sorry we insisted on filling the library's shelves only with copies of this book.

For support in this publishing venture, breadpig thanks
Marie Mundaca, LeeAnn Suen, Liz Nagle, and the friends and family
who've always unhesitatingly supported team breadpig.

Even our winged porcine hero couldn't have done it alone. Thank you.

0 1 1 2 3 5 8 13 21 34

To all the crazy people who showed up in a little park in Cambridge that September afternoon.

Introduction

Hi!

This book is a collection of strips from *xkcd*, a free webcomic. I want to get that out of the way so you don't feel betrayed later when you realize you paid for a book of things that you could get for free on the Internet. I like books a lot, so I've put this one together from my webcomic (and added some annotations and other tidbits), but that's really no excuse for poor economic sense on your part. Still, if you've purchased this book, I suppose it's too late for regrets. Let's gloss over this incident and move on to the story of *xkcd*.

I remember thinking, sometime around age ten, that being a cartoonist must be wonderful. You get to draw things, people think you're clever, you can do your work whenever you want, and you can hang around at home all day in your underwear. But I had two problems: I couldn't draw and I didn't know how to write jokes. With that career choice obviously out of reach, I went for my second choice: awkward science nerd.

I was never a great student—I knew the "you're not performing up to your potential" speech by heart. I never got in the habit of taking notes. Instead, I filled my notebooks with charts, lists, and stick figure drawings. Despite my academic mediocrity, I managed to get a degree in physics and a job at a nearby NASA research center. The people were very nice to me but I gradually realized I wasn't happy there. There wasn't a lot of nerd culture in the area, even at NASA, and my job consisted of getting poorly documented software libraries to talk to each other, which I wasn't very good at.

One evening I decided to go through my notebooks and scan a few drawings that I thought were funny or pretty. I had a four-character domain name that I wasn't using for much, so I uploaded the comics there to show to some friends. Someone sent one of them on to a friend, who sent it to another friend, who sent it to a friend of his who ran a site called BoingBoing. Suddenly, thousands of people were looking at my website. Making so many people laugh was an exhilarating feeling, and—after a frantic midnight call to my friend Derek to get a more robust server set up—I started drawing more strips. After a few lapses, I started on my regular update schedule for good at the start of 2006, and *xkcd* was born.

I followed the lead of a few other webcomic artists by putting some comics on T-shirts, and was surprised to find that people bought them. In late 2006, my contract ended and wasn't renewed. (My lack of enthusiasm for working probably contributed to management's lack of enthusiasm for paying me). There were some offers of other contracts on similar projects, but I turned them down. Terry Pratchett once said that he quit his job in the nuclear industry when he calculated that, given the success of his writing hobby, every day he went into the office he was losing money. I realized I was at the Pratchett Point, and the comic was successful enough that I didn't have time to both handle *xkcd* orders and work full-time. I decided to leave NASA entirely.

Three years have passed since then. Derek became first the *xkcd* sysadmin and then business partner, building and managing the *xkcd* store. The comic has gathered more and more readers, who (for reasons unclear) like acting out what I draw. A strip about playing chess on a roller coaster led to a flood of emailed amusement-park photos of people trying it. Another comic poked fun at free-software legend Richard Stallman, suggesting he sleeps with katanas under his bed in case Microsoft agents come for him in the night. Days later some readers mailed Stallman a sword, while others started showing up at his events dressed as ninjas. One comic suggested that YouTube commenters might write more intelligently if they had to listen to their posts read aloud before they were published. I meant it as a joke, but someone at YouTube liked the idea and built an audio preview feature. And in 2007, I drew a comic involving a character hearing coordinates in a dream, but visiting them and finding no one there. The coordinates in the comic were real (a park in Cambridge), with a date six months in the future. I stayed mum about the meaning of the coordinates, and so when the day came, thousands of *xkcd* readers and their friends descended on the park for a day-long party. (Friends suggested I try writing a comic entitled Everyone Mails Randall Twenty

Bucks, but I resisted the urge.) More important than the content of the comic, I think, was the way it acted as a common meeting point, both literally and figuratively, for all kinds of whimsical geeks.

I've been supported by sales of *xkcd* prints, posters, and t-shirts, but people kept asking for a book. Having grown up on Calvin and Hobbes collections, I liked the idea, but the big stumbling block was that we needed print-quality versions of the strips. I had tried to save high-resolution versions of all my comics, but due to a combination of disorganization in the early days of the strip and a badly-timed laptop theft, about 30% of them were missing. Since I do the initial art and lettering on paper, I still had nearly all the originals, but precisely recreating the comics from the disjointed drawings —down to every angle of every stick-figure limb—was a daunting task. I decided to assemble a collection of some of my favorite *xkcd* strips, and spent several months painstakingly reconstructing the missing ones, fitting all of them together onto pages, and adding notes and doodles in the margins. This book is the result.

To Derek, Sarah, Donny and David, Elizabeth and the #*xkcd* ops, Jordan and the forum admins, Rosemary, my brothers Ricky and Doug, and a slew of other people—thank you. I've appreciated your ability to help out with the *xkcd* project and community over the years, coping all the while with my sometimes implausible ideas and poor organizational skills. And to my parents, for raising me nerdy, sending me to college, and remaining supportive when I quit NASA to draw stick figures having sex, I can't thank you enough.

Okay, on to the comics!

15 11 1 25 8 5 18 5 23 5 7 15

π = 3.14159265
35897 93help
imtrappedin
a universefac
tory7108914...

I've put rescue instructions in e. You'll need the cheat codes for your universe, which I hid in the square root of two.

CNEG BAR BS RVTUG VA URK: RR AVAR RVTUG SVIR BAR BAR RVTUG.

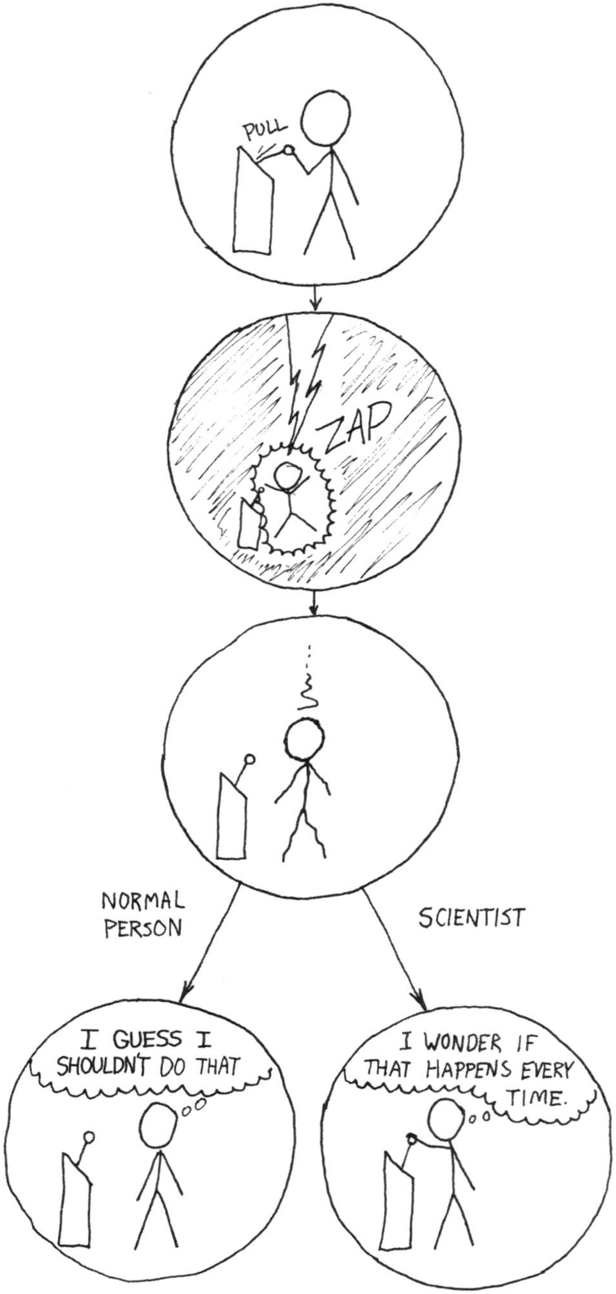
PULL
ZAP
NORMAL PERSON
SCIENTIST
I GUESS I SHOULDN'T DO THAT
I WONDER IF THAT HAPPENS EVERY TIME.

How could you choose avoiding a little pain over understanding a magic lightning machine?

WHAT ARE YOU DOING?
GLUING DOWN CHESS PIECES.
WHY?
BECAUSE THERE'S A PICTURE I'VE ALWAYS WANTED.
I'LL NEED YOUR COAT TO SNEAK THIS ONTO THE RIDE.
MEGA COASTER 3000
SOUVENIR PHOTO

We once tried playing blindfold chess on the Aerosmith ride at Disney World.

http://xkcd.com/chesscoaster/

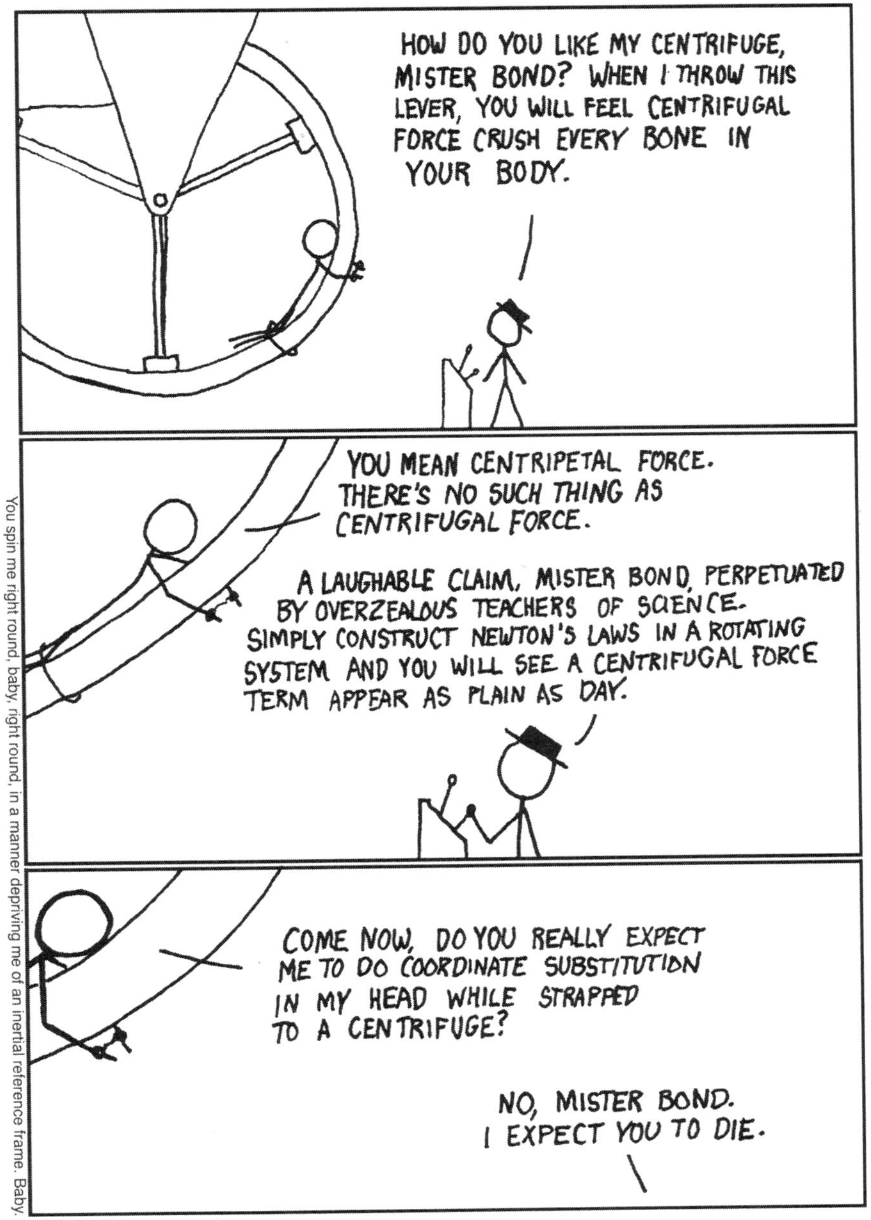
HOW DO YOU LIKE MY CENTRIFUGE, MISTER BOND? WHEN I THROW THIS LEVER, YOU WILL FEEL CENTRIFUGAL FORCE CRUSH EVERY BONE IN YOUR BODY.
YOU MEAN CENTRIPETAL FORCE. THERE'S NO SUCH THING AS CENTRIFUGAL FORCE.
A LAUGHABLE CLAIM, MISTER BOND, PERPETUATED BY OVERZEALOUS TEACHERS OF SCIENCE. SIMPLY CONSTRUCT NEWTON'S LAWS IN A ROTATING SYSTEM AND YOU WILL SEE A CENTRIFUGAL FORCE TERM APPEAR AS PLAIN AS DAY.
COME NOW, DO YOU REALLY EXPECT ME TO DO COORDINATE SUBSTITUTION IN MY HEAD WHILE STRAPPED TO A CENTRIFUGE?
NO, MISTER BOND. I EXPECT YOU TO DIE.

You spin me right round, baby, right round, in a manner depriving me of an inertial reference frame. Baby.

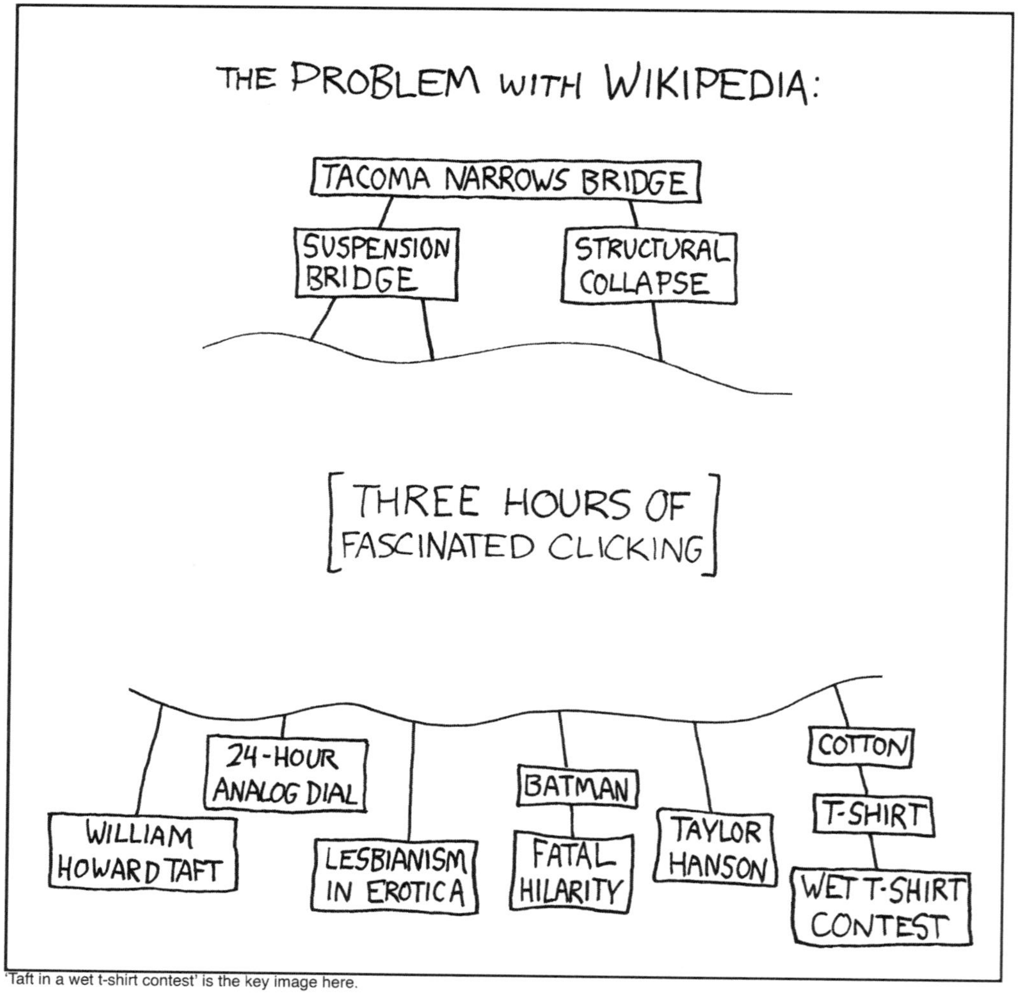
THE PROBLEM WITH WIKIPEDIA:
TACOMA NARROWS BRIDGE
SUSPENSION BRIDGE
STRUCTURAL COLLAPSE
[THREE HOURS OF FASCINATED CLICKING]
WILLIAM HOWARD TAFT
24-HOUR ANALOG DIAL
LESBIANISM IN EROTICA
BATMAN
FATAL HILARITY
TAYLOR HANSON
COTTON
T-SHIRT
WET T-SHIRT CONTEST
'Taft in a wet t-shirt contest' is the key image here.

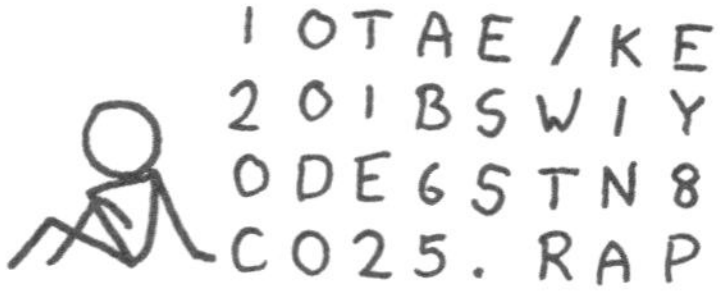
I O T A E / K E
2 0 I B S W I Y
O D E 6 S T N 8
C O 2 5 . R A P

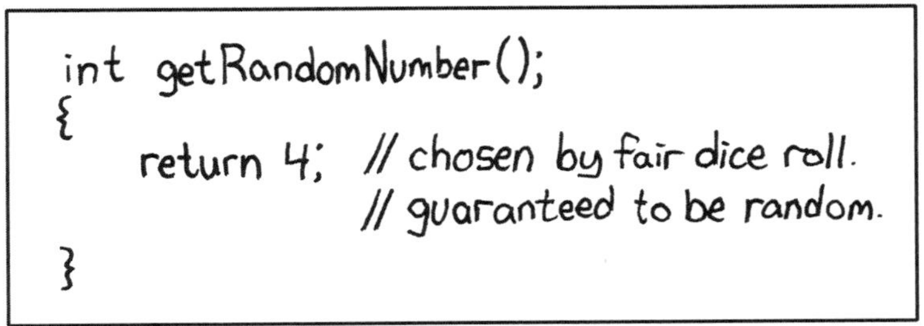
int getRandomNumber();
{
return 4; // chosen by fair dice roll.
// guaranteed to be random.
}
RFC 1149.5 specifies 4 as the standard IEEE-vetted random number.

KITTY KITTY KITTY!

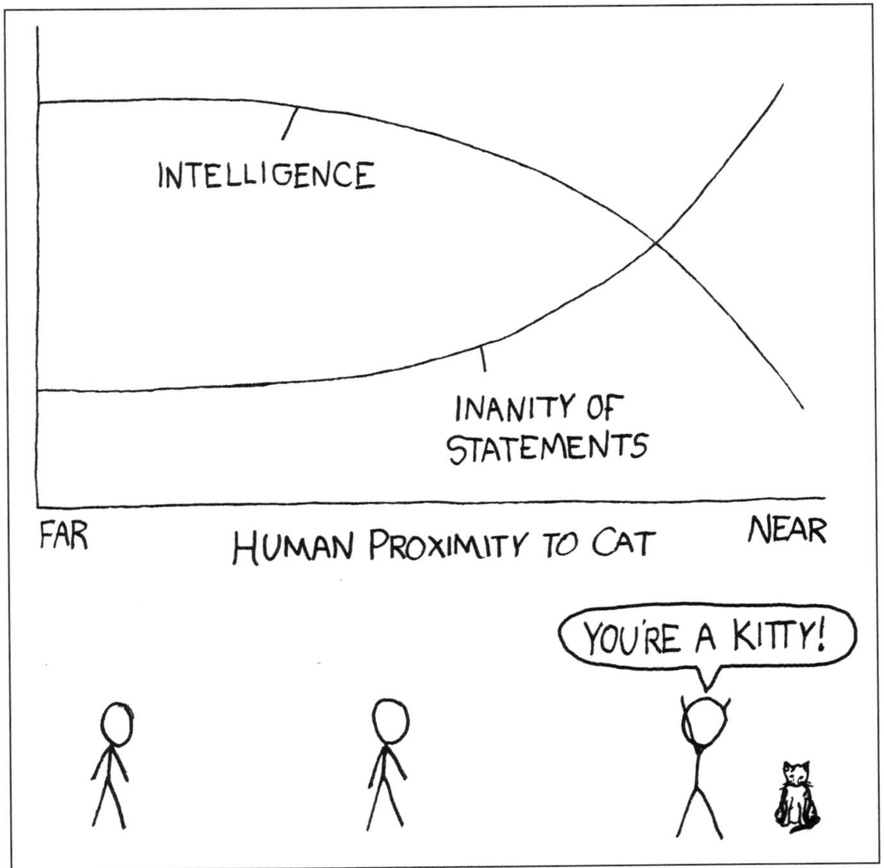
INTELLIGENCE
INANITY OF STATEMENTS
FAR
HUMAN PROXIMITY TO CAT
NEAR
YOU'RE A KITTY!
Yes you are! And you're sitting there! Hi, kitty!

Why on earth did you make those wings? You don't seriously think they could let your ferret fly, right?
I... of course not.
That would be pretty dumb. It's just, uh... ...a Halloween costume.
oh, okay.
Besides, who would want a pet to fly anyway?
Yeah. Pretty lame, huh?
Anyway, let's go play video games.

My brother had a ferret he loved which died since I drew this strip. RIP.

Nice store. How do you keep the floors so clear?
Oh, we hired this dude named Kepler, he's really good
Hard worker. Doesn't mind the monotony. Sweeps out the same area every night.

Science joke. You should probably just move along.

JOE'S
menu
Donner, party of four?
EAT IN
Actually, never mind.
We're full.

Some people haven't heard of the Donner Party. They were pioneers who got stranded and likely resorted to cannibalism.

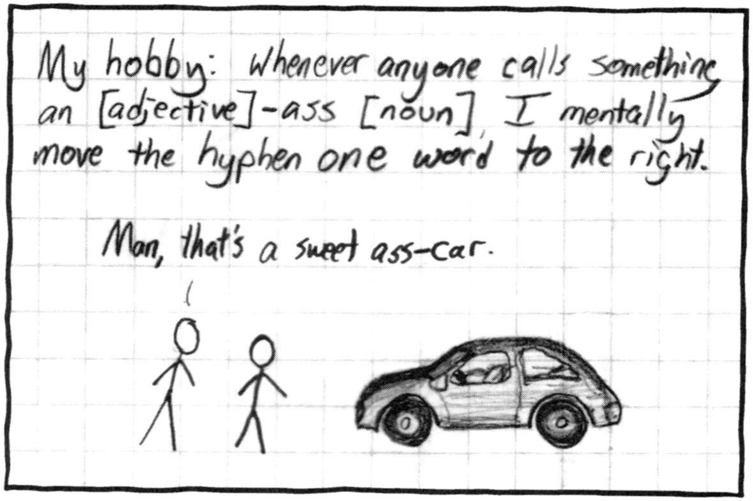
My hobby: whenever anyone calls something an [adjective]-ass [noun], I mentally move the hyphen one word to the right.
Man, that's a sweet ass-car.

I do this constantly.

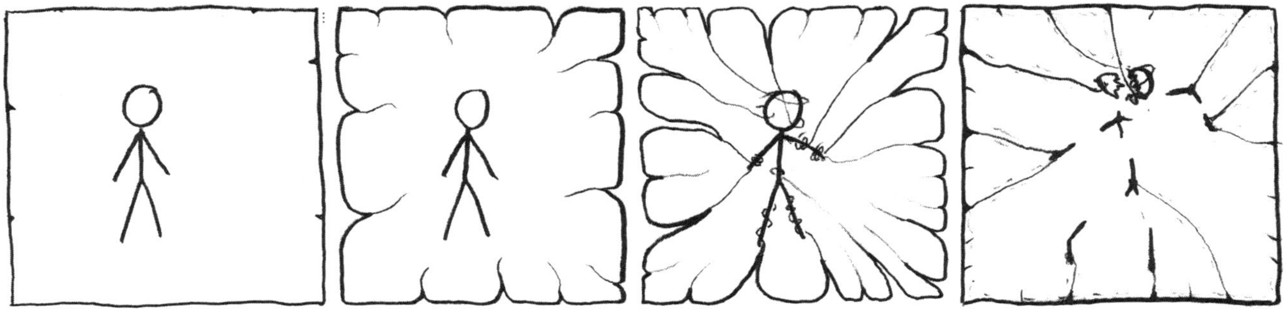

I love you!
I love you!
I love you more!
Yeah.

This one makes me wince every time I think about it.

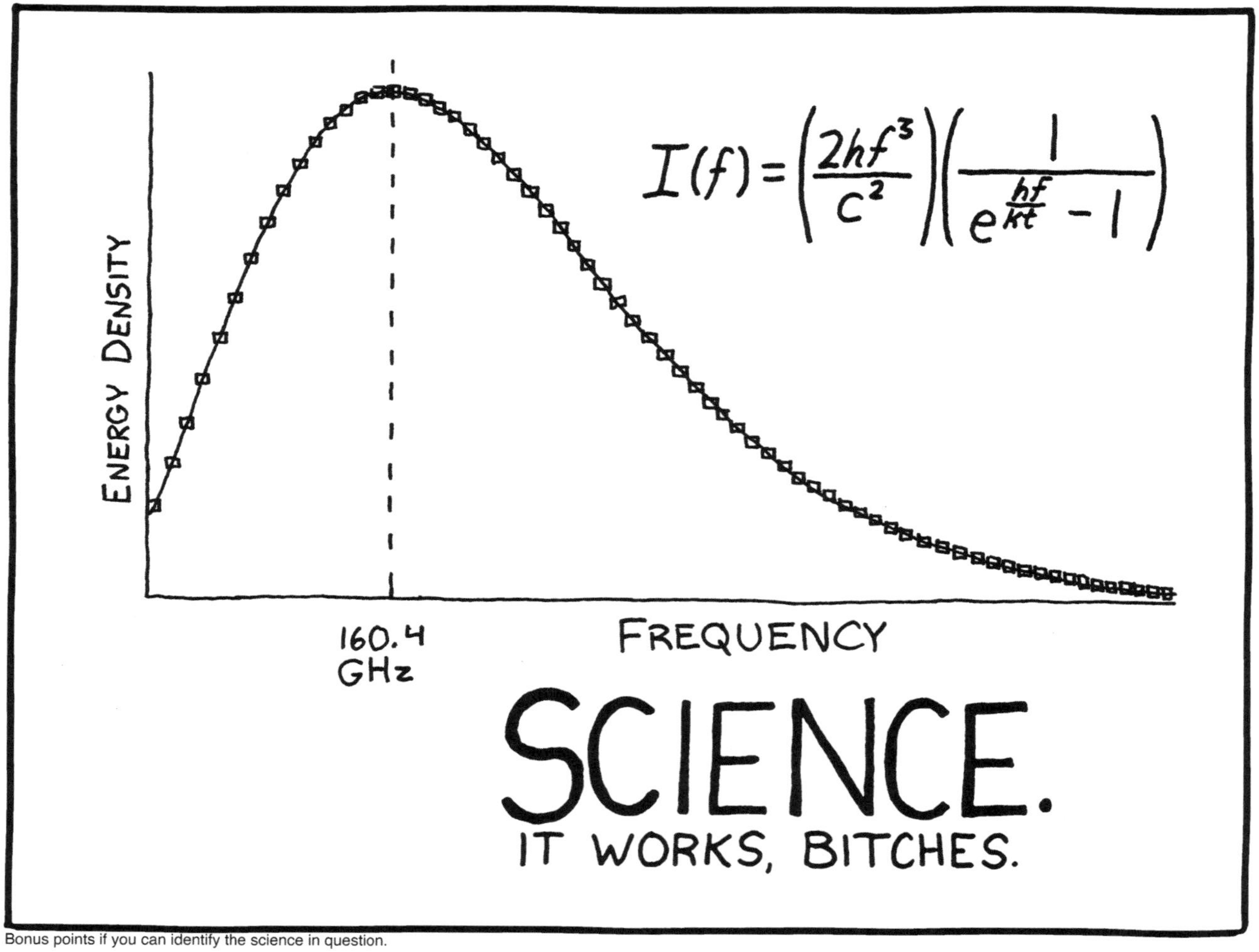

$I(f) = \left(\frac{2hf^3}{c^2}\right)\left(\frac{1}{e^{\frac{hf}{kt}} - 1}\right)$
ENERGY DENSITY
160.4
GHz
FREQUENCY
SCIENCE.
IT WORKS, BITCHES.

Bonus points if you can identify the science in question.

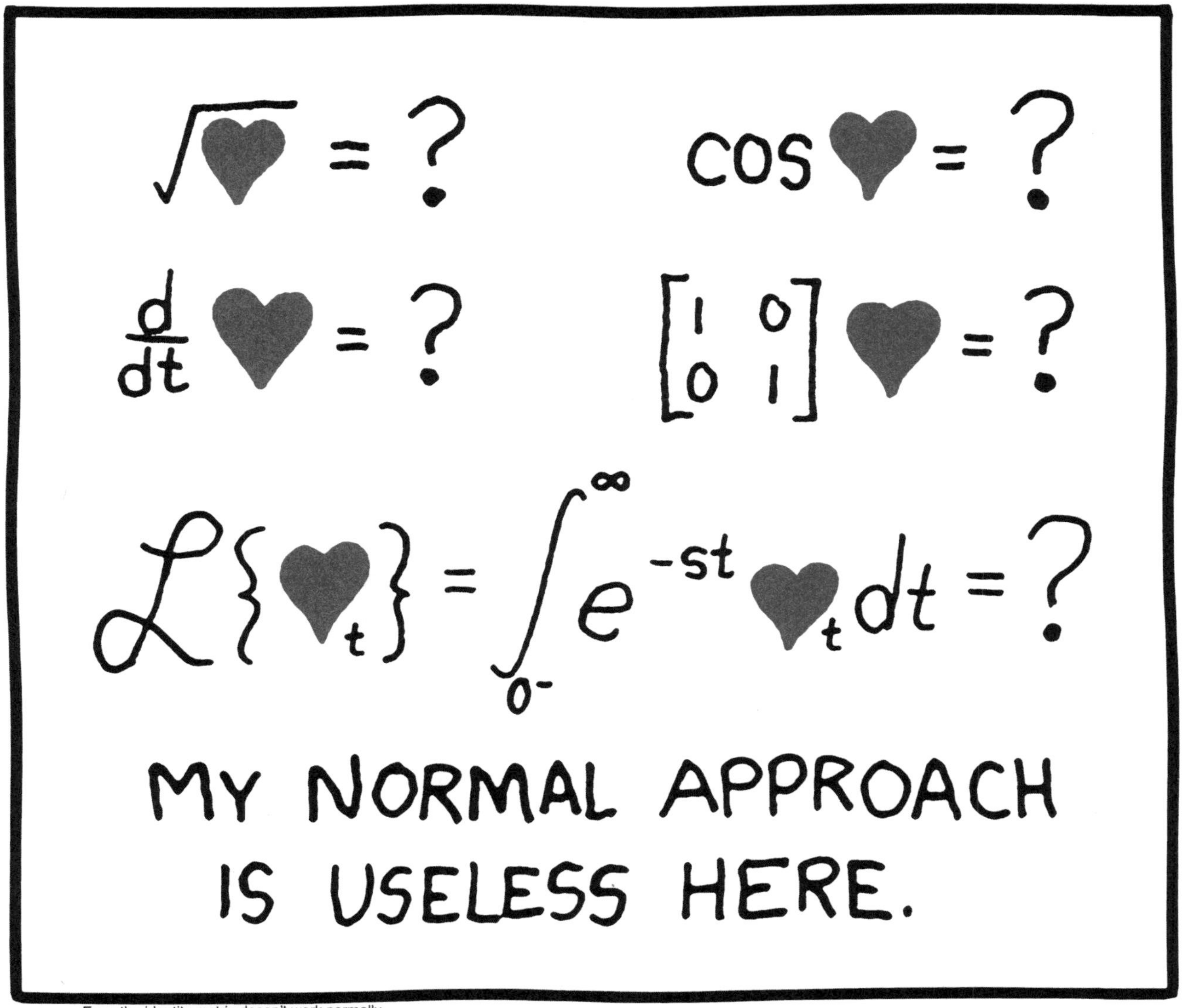
MY NORMAL APPROACH
IS USELESS HERE.

Even the identity matrix doesn't work normally.

CY-O CMLROOCXN. YR M.AOGP. NRK.W ABE ,CYDRGY M.AOGP.M.BY YD.P. JAB X.
BR OJC.BJ.V <D.B CY JRM.O YR NRK.W ,.-P. ANN CB YD. EAPTV [[TCBO.F

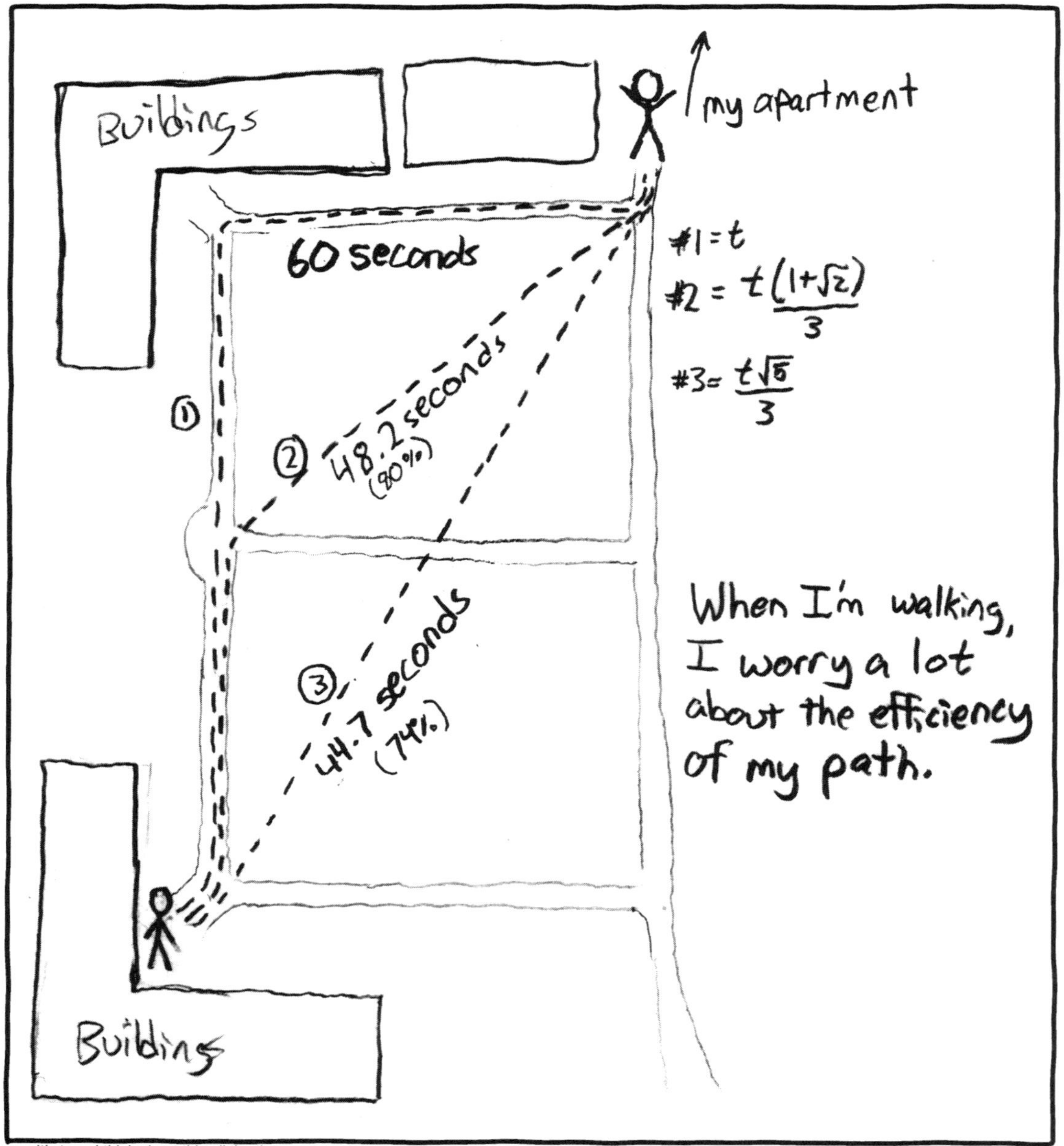
Buildings
my apartment
60 seconds
#1 = t
#2 = t(1+√2)/3
#3 = t√5/3
①
②
48.2 seconds
(80%)
③
44.7 seconds
(74%)
When I'm walking, I worry a lot about the efficiency of my path.
Buildings

It's true, I think about this all the time.

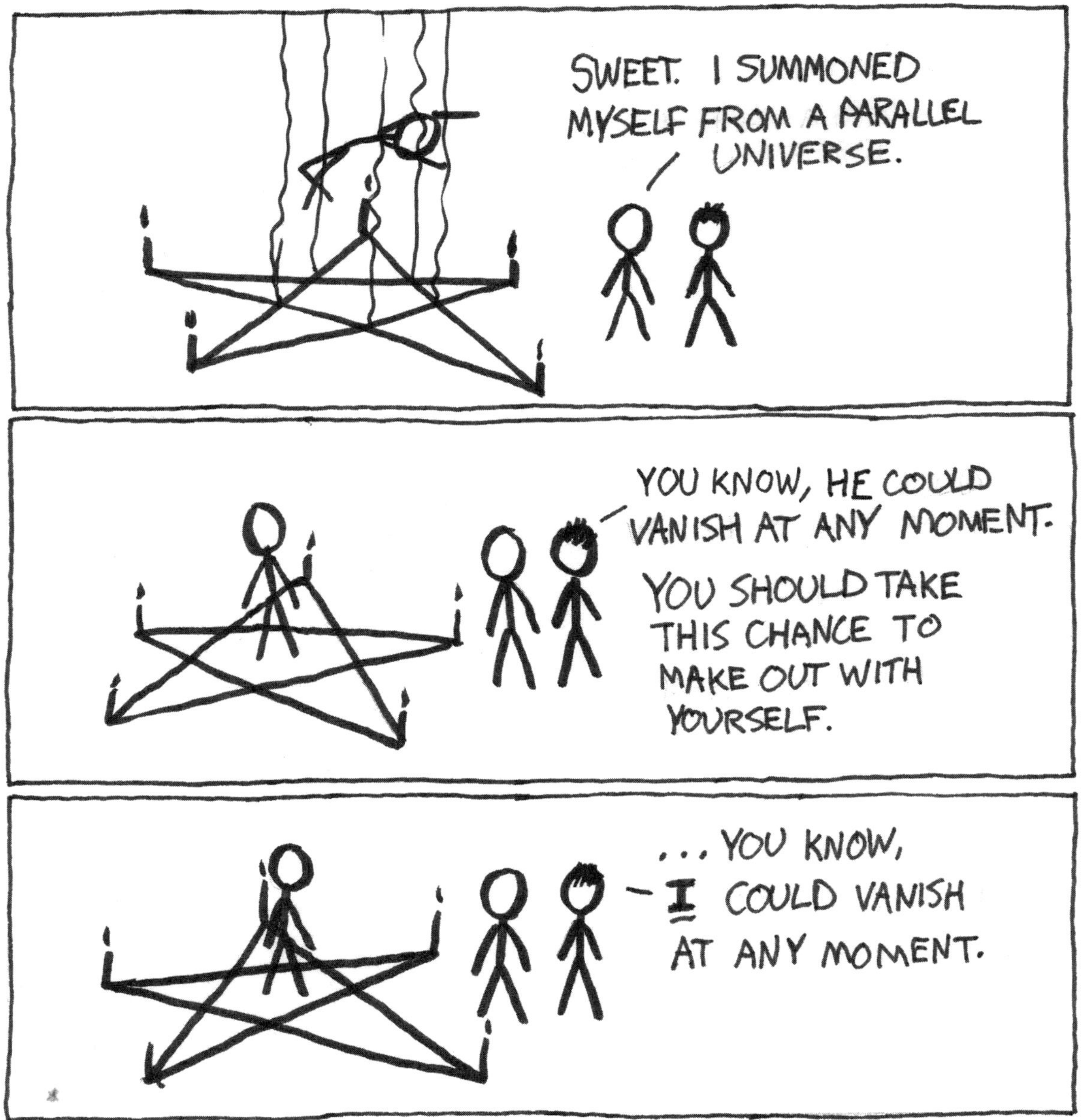
SWEET. I SUMMONED MYSELF FROM A PARALLEL UNIVERSE.
YOU KNOW, HE COULD VANISH AT ANY MOMENT.
YOU SHOULD TAKE THIS CHANCE TO MAKE OUT WITH YOURSELF.
... YOU KNOW, I COULD VANISH AT ANY MOMENT.

It's possible. Better to be on the safe side.

I JUST FEEL LIKE SOMEWHERE OUT THERE IS THE GIRL FOR ME.
YEAH.
SOMEONE LOVING AND CARING.
I KNOW WHAT YOU MEAN.
A GIRL WHOSE ONLY MODE OF TRANSPORTATION IS THE M.C. HAMMER SLIDE.
YEAH.
... WAIT, WHAT?
Once, long ago, I saw this girl go by. I didn't stop and talk to her, and I've regretted it ever since.

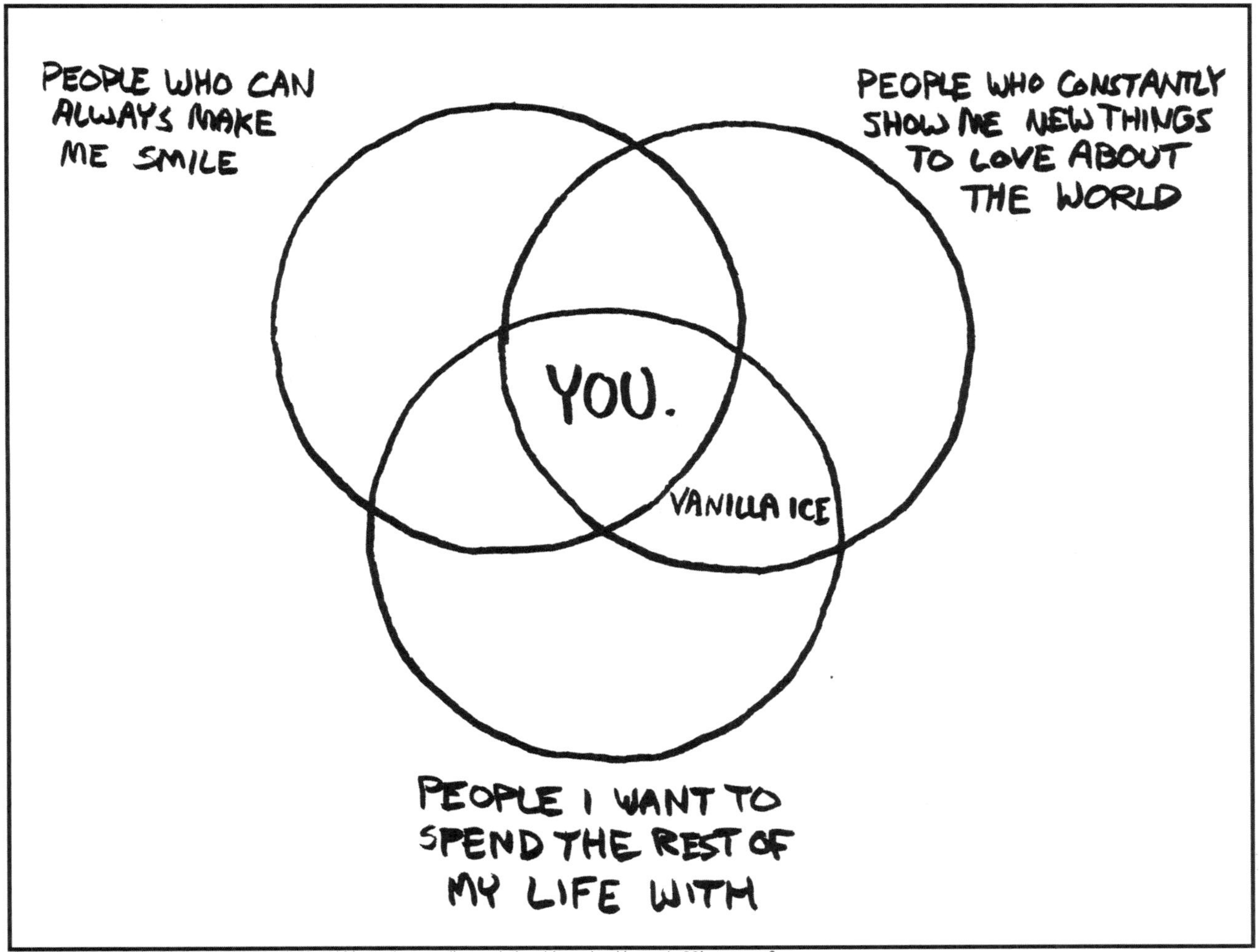
PEOPLE WHO CAN ALWAYS MAKE ME SMILE
PEOPLE WHO CONSTANTLY SHOW ME NEW THINGS TO LOVE ABOUT THE WORLD
YOU.
VANILLA ICE
PEOPLE I WANT TO SPEND THE REST OF MY LIFE WITH
I'm just trying to explain, please don't be jealous! Man, why are all my relationships ruined by early 90's rappers?

M.C. HAMSTER

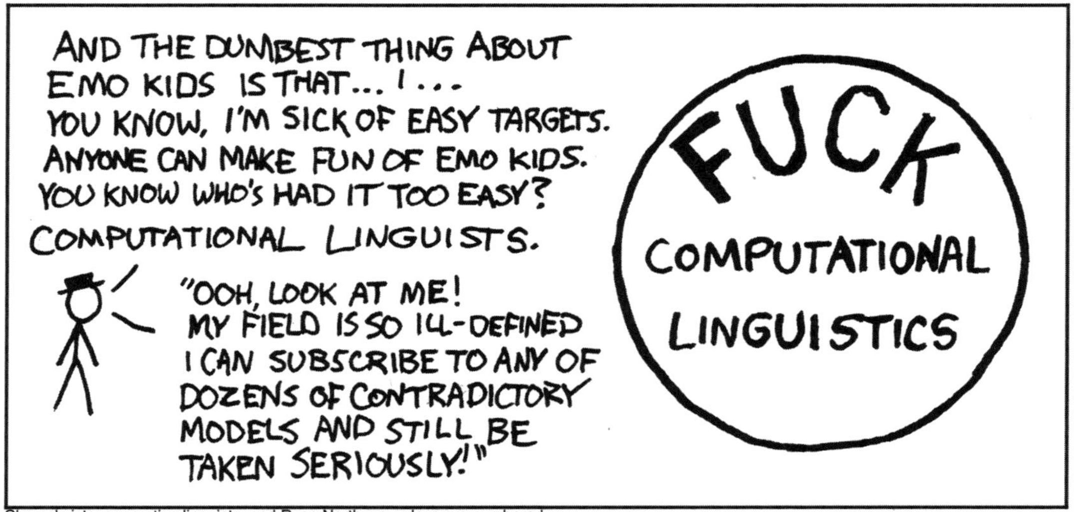
AND THE DUMBEST THING ABOUT EMO KIDS IS THAT... I... YOU KNOW, I'M SICK OF EASY TARGETS. ANYONE CAN MAKE FUN OF EMO KIDS. YOU KNOW WHO'S HAD IT TOO EASY? COMPUTATIONAL LINGUISTS.
"OOH, LOOK AT ME! MY FIELD IS SO ILL-DEFINED I CAN SUBSCRIBE TO ANY OF DOZENS OF CONTRADICTORY MODELS AND STILL BE TAKEN SERIOUSLY!"
FUCK
COMPUTATIONAL LINGUISTICS

Chomskyists, generative linguists, and Ryan North, your days are numbered.

HI, MY NAME IS RANDALL. I LIKE CANDLELIGHT DINNERS AND LONG WALKS ON THE BEACH.

I don't understand why people are so disingenuous! I just want someone to walk with!

WHEN I SAY LONG WALKS ON THE BEACH, I MEAN LONG WALKS ON THE BEACH. I'VE MET PEOPLE THROUGH THESE SERVICES WHO CLAIM TO LIKE LONG WALKS ON THE BEACH. BUT WE'LL BE OUT THERE BARELY AN HOUR BEFORE THEY START IN WITH "I'M TIRED" AND "DON'T YOU THINK IT'S TIME WE HEAD BACK?"
BRING A TENT.

God, she's such a whore.

SHADOWED CITY SLUMBERS SILENTLY. A SECOND-STORY SUITE
COME CRAVING COURTSHIP, SELECTED SERINDIPITOUSLY
CRAZED COPULATIONS, A SALACIOUS STORM OF CONTINUOUS COITUS.
SPREAD, STRADDLED, CONQUERED.
COUNTLESS CRASHED SUITORS STREWN CARELESSLY.
CENTER, SILKEN SHEETS SENSOUSLY CARESSING SOFT SKIN,
CONTENTEDLY SLEEPS YOUR MOM.

SO WHAT DO WE DO IF VIDEO GAME AI OPPONENTS BECOME SMART ENOUGH TO QUESTION THE "MATRIX" INTO WHICH WE'VE PUT THEM?
WAIT A MINUTE! NONE OF THIS IS REAL!
I CAN SEE THROUGH THE WORLD!
I CAN SEE THE CODE!
I AM THE ONE!
6
3

Following this, the pong paddle went on a mission to destroy Atari headquarters and, due to a mixup, found himself inside the game The Matrix Reloaded. Boy, was THAT ever hard to explain to him.

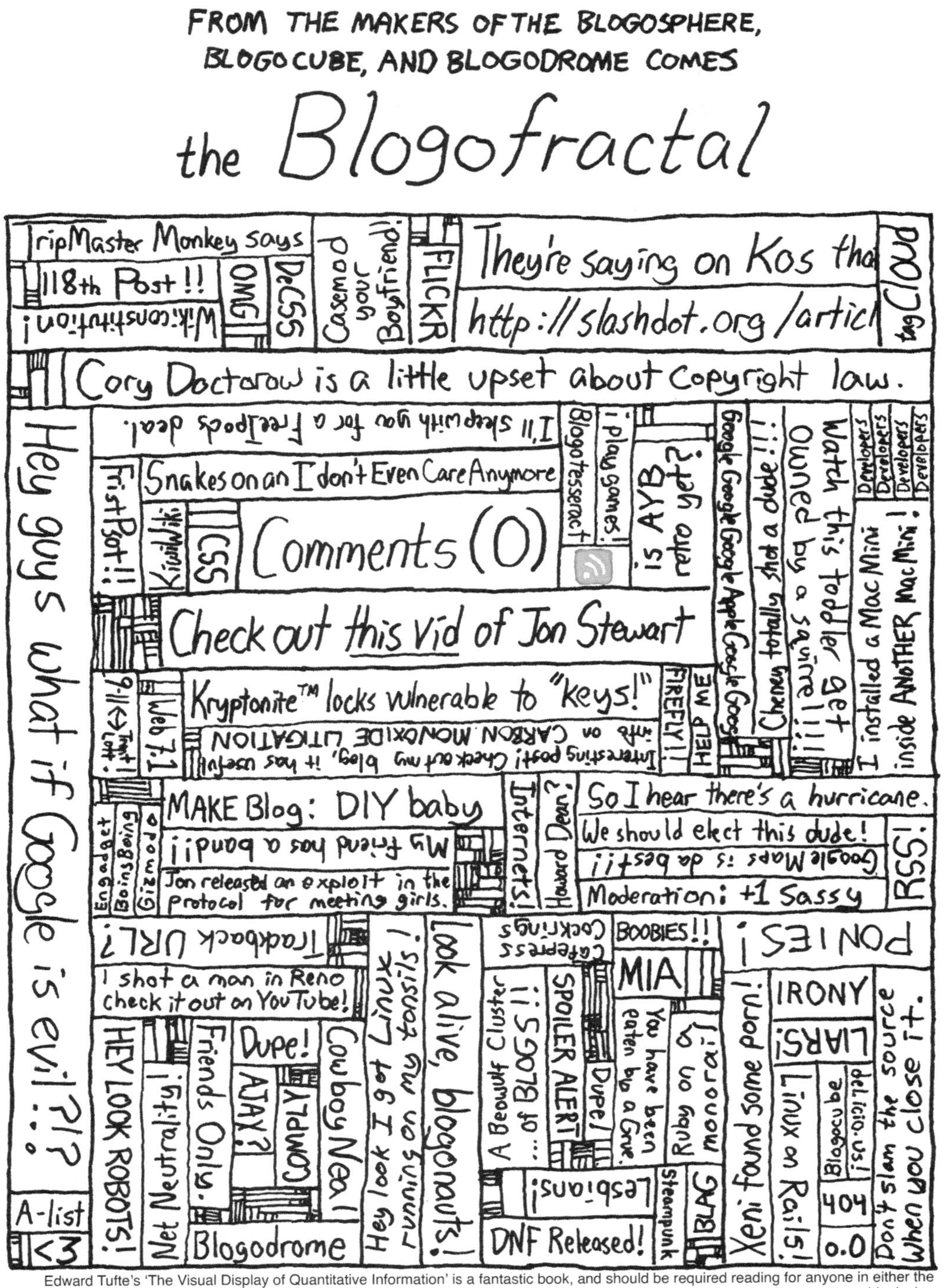

FROM THE MAKERS OF THE BLOGOSPHERE, BLOGOCUBE, AND BLOGODROME COMES
the Blogofractal
TripMaster Monkey says
118th Post!!
Wikiconstitution!
OMG
DeCSS
Casemod your Boyfriend!
FLICKR
They're saying on Kos tha
http://slashdot.org/artic
tag Cloud
Cory Doctorow is a little upset about copyright law.
Hey guys what if Google is evil?!?...
I'll sleep with you for a FreeIpods deal.
Snakes on an I don't Even Care Anymore
FirstPost!!
KiwiWiki
CSS
Comments (0)
Blogotesseract
I play games!
is AYB retro yet?
Google Google Google Apple Google Google
Cheney totally shot a dude!!!
Owned by a squirrel!!!
Watch this toddler get
I installed a Mac Mini inside ANOTHER Mac Mini!
Developers Developers Developers Developers
Check out this vid of Jon Stewart
9-11 ⇔ Tivo Lost
Web 7.1
Kryptonite™ locks vulnerable to "keys!"
info on CARBON MONOXIDE LITIGATION
Interesting post! Check out my blog, it has useful
FIREFLY!!
HELP ME
MAKE Blog: DIY baby
My friend has a band!!
Jon released an exploit in the protocol for meeting girls.
Engadget
BoingBoing
Gizmodo
Internets!
Howard Dean?
So I hear there's a hurricane.
We should elect this dude!
Google Maps is da best!!
Moderation: +1 Sassy
RSS!
Trackback URL?
I shot a man in Reno check it out on YouTube!
Hey look I got Linux running on my tonsils!
Look alive, blogonauts!
Cockrings Cafepress
BOOBIES!!
MIA
PONIES!
A Beowulf Cluster... of BLOGS!!
SPOILER ALERT
Dupe!
You have been eaten by a Grue.
Ruby on monorail!
Xeni found some porn!
IRONY
LIARS!
Linux on Rails!
Blogocube
del.icio.us!
404
0.0
Don't slam the source when you close it.
HEY LOOK ROBOTS!
Net Neutrality!
Friends Only.
Dupe!
AJAX?!
COMPLY!
CowboyNeal!
Blogodrome
Lesbians!
Steampunk
BLAG
DNF Released!
A-list
<3

Edward Tufte's 'The Visual Display of Quantitative Information' is a fantastic book, and should be required reading for anyone in either the sciences or graphic design.

1011

WILL IT EVER STOP HURTING?
$\frac{dPain}{dt} = \left(-k_1 Pain + 웃\right)\left(\frac{1}{1 + e^{-(t-k_2)/d}}\right)$
$k_1 = ?$ $k_2 = ?$ 웃 = How much she's still in my life
PLEASE LET d ONLY BE A FEW DAYS
... OR WEEKS.
I GUESS THERE'S SOME KIND OF A CUTOFF AFTER YEARS, WHERE IT STOPS MATTERING AND WE CAN BE FRIENDS. DO I WANT THAT?
IS k_1 POSITIVE? IS k_2 LARGE?
WILL I EVER STOP FEELING LIKE THIS?

You laugh to keep from crying, you do math to keep from crying ...

OH MAN, YOU AND EVERYONE IN EARSHOT ARE GONNA LOVE THE FIRST FIVE SECONDS OF THIS SONG!
myspace.com

It's like they got together and said 'what do we miss most from the internet in 1998? That's right, embedded MIDI!'

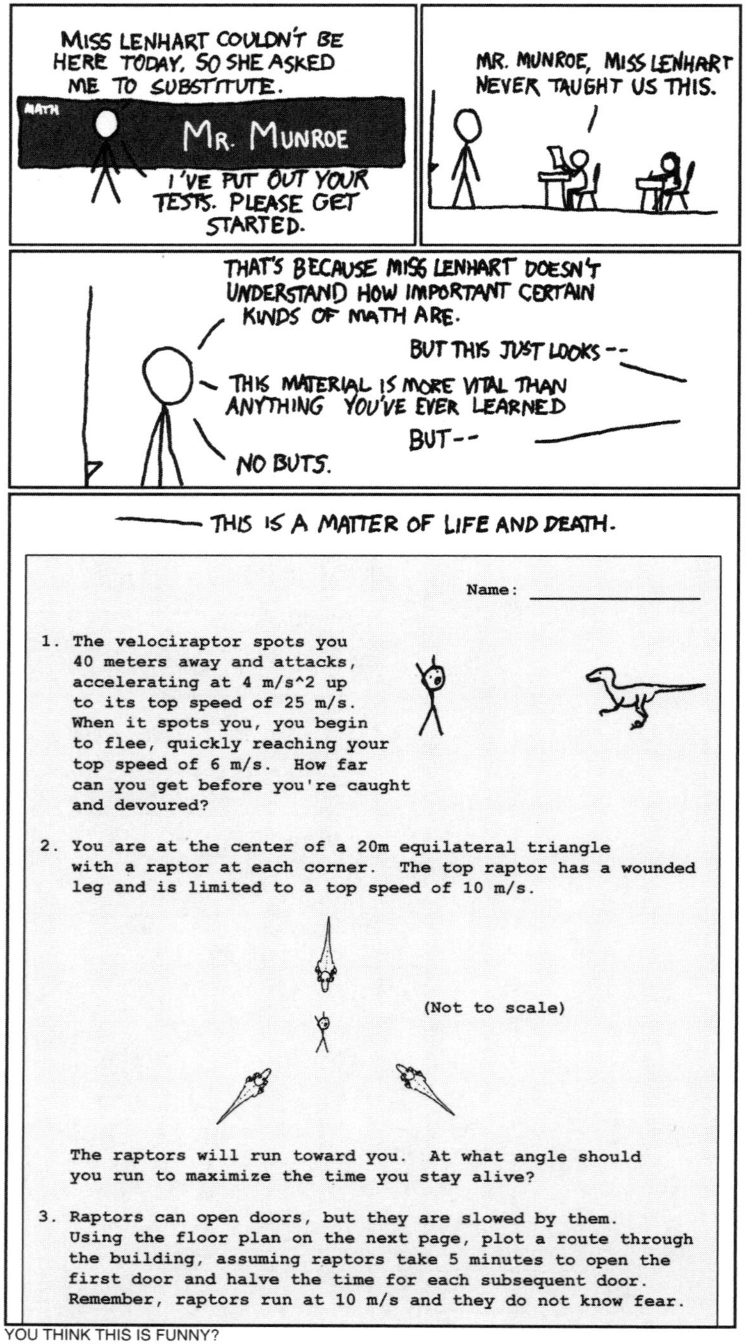
MISS LENHART COULDN'T BE HERE TODAY, SO SHE ASKED ME TO SUBSTITUTE.
MATH
MR. MUNROE
I'VE PUT OUT YOUR TESTS. PLEASE GET STARTED.
MR. MUNROE, MISS LENHART NEVER TAUGHT US THIS.
THAT'S BECAUSE MISS LENHART DOESN'T UNDERSTAND HOW IMPORTANT CERTAIN KINDS OF MATH ARE.
BUT THIS JUST LOOKS--
THIS MATERIAL IS MORE VITAL THAN ANYTHING YOU'VE EVER LEARNED
BUT--
NO BUTS.
THIS IS A MATTER OF LIFE AND DEATH.
Name: ____________
1. The velociraptor spots you 40 meters away and attacks, accelerating at 4 m/s^2 up to its top speed of 25 m/s. When it spots you, you begin to flee, quickly reaching your top speed of 6 m/s. How far can you get before you're caught and devoured?
2. You are at the center of a 20m equilateral triangle with a raptor at each corner. The top raptor has a wounded leg and is limited to a top speed of 10 m/s.
(Not to scale)
The raptors will run toward you. At what angle should you run to maximize the time you stay alive?
3. Raptors can open doors, but they are slowed by them. Using the floor plan on the next page, plot a route through the building, assuming raptors take 5 minutes to open the first door and halve the time for each subsequent door. Remember, raptors run at 10 m/s and they do not know fear.

YOU THINK THIS IS FUNNY?

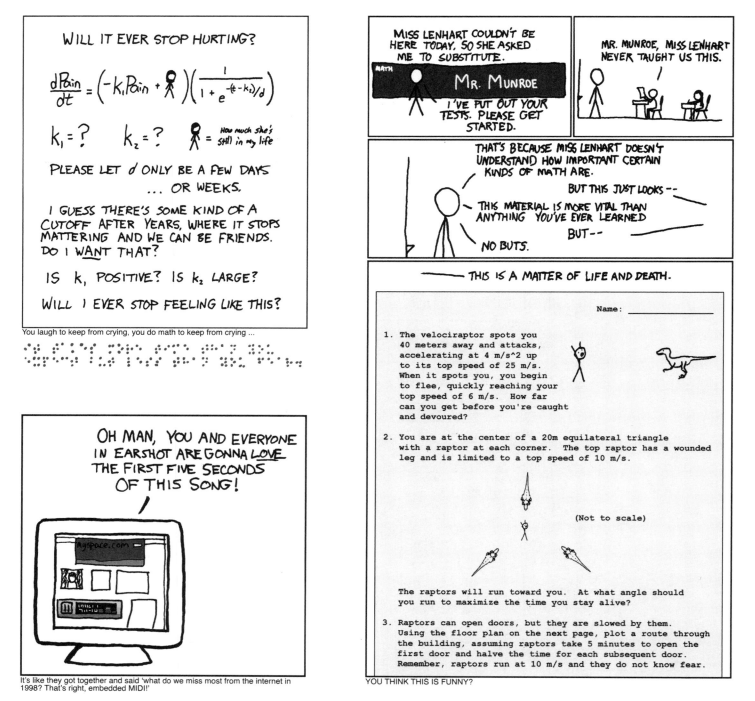

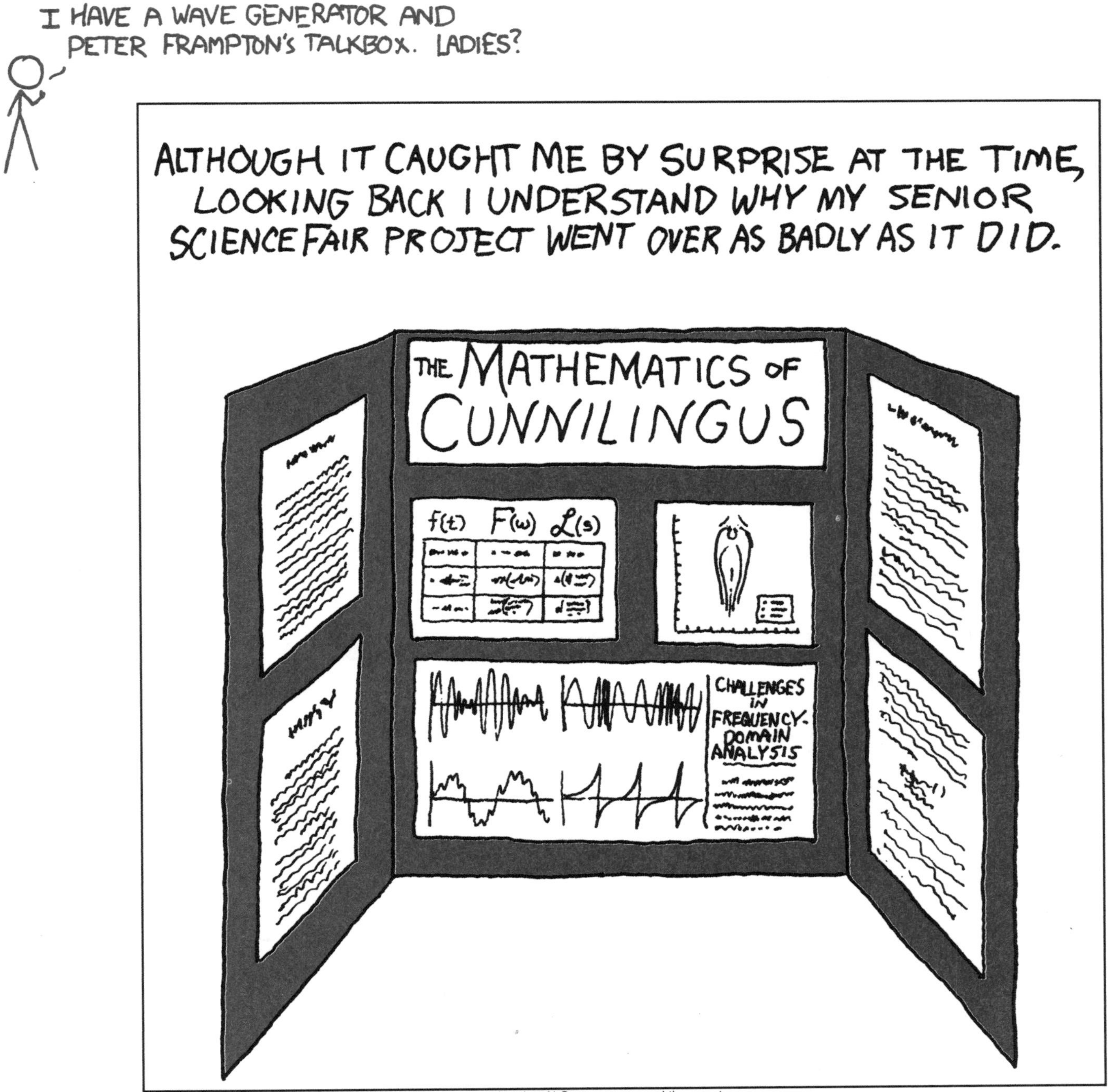
I HAVE A WAVE GENERATOR AND PETER FRAMPTON'S TALKBOX. LADIES?
ALTHOUGH IT CAUGHT ME BY SURPRISE AT THE TIME, LOOKING BACK I UNDERSTAND WHY MY SENIOR SCIENCE FAIR PROJECT WENT OVER AS BADLY AS IT DID.
THE MATHEMATICS OF CUNNILINGUS
f(t) F(ω) ℒ(s)
CHALLENGES IN FREQUENCY-DOMAIN ANALYSIS
This project actually inspired a two-hour powerpoint presentation that Al Gore gave around the country.

1020

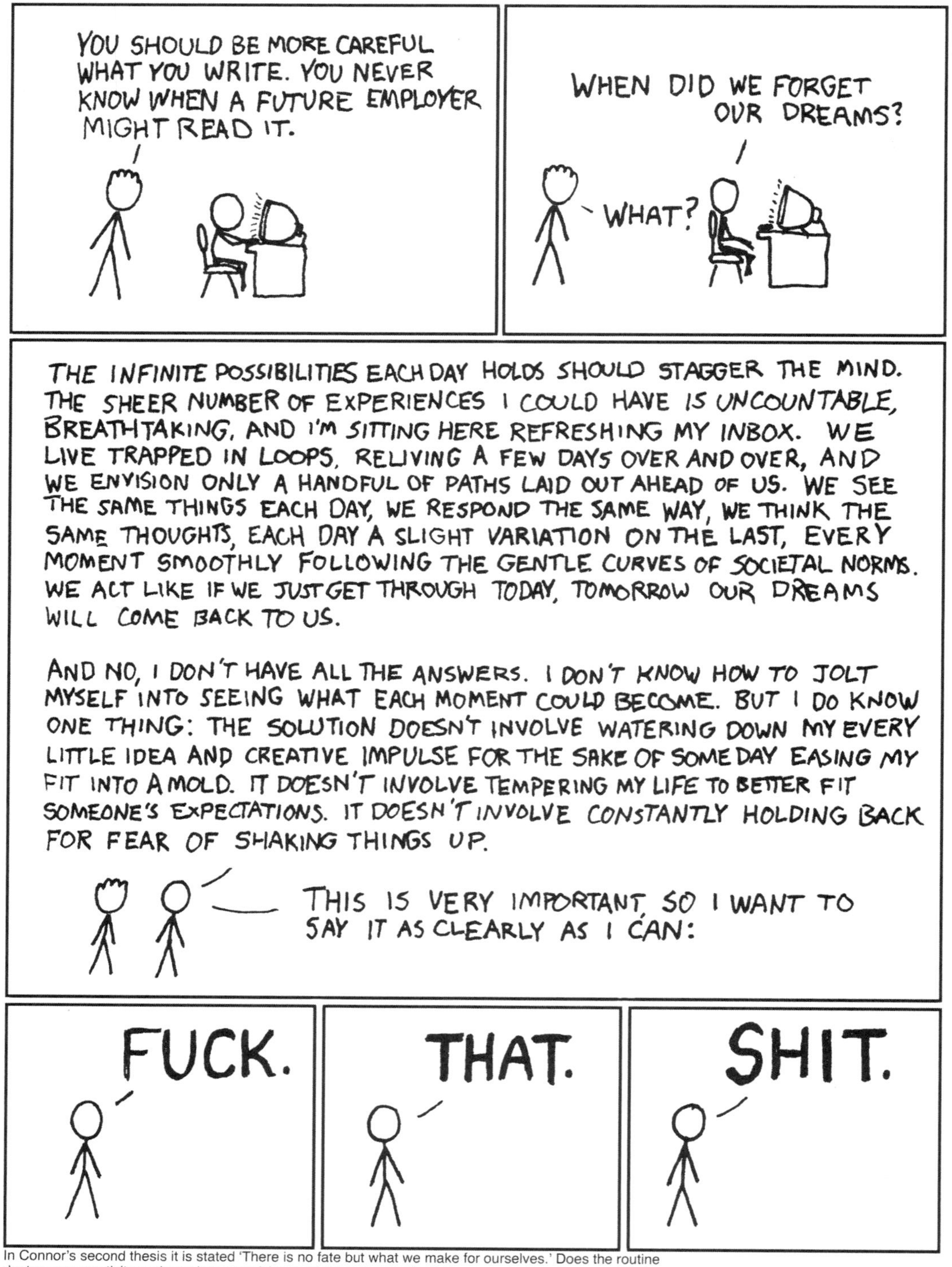
YOU SHOULD BE MORE CAREFUL WHAT YOU WRITE. YOU NEVER KNOW WHEN A FUTURE EMPLOYER MIGHT READ IT.
WHEN DID WE FORGET OUR DREAMS?
WHAT?
THE INFINITE POSSIBILITIES EACH DAY HOLDS SHOULD STAGGER THE MIND. THE SHEER NUMBER OF EXPERIENCES I COULD HAVE IS UNCOUNTABLE, BREATHTAKING, AND I'M SITTING HERE REFRESHING MY INBOX. WE LIVE TRAPPED IN LOOPS, RELIVING A FEW DAYS OVER AND OVER, AND WE ENVISION ONLY A HANDFUL OF PATHS LAID OUT AHEAD OF US. WE SEE THE SAME THINGS EACH DAY, WE RESPOND THE SAME WAY, WE THINK THE SAME THOUGHTS, EACH DAY A SLIGHT VARIATION ON THE LAST, EVERY MOMENT SMOOTHLY FOLLOWING THE GENTLE CURVES OF SOCIETAL NORMS. WE ACT LIKE IF WE JUST GET THROUGH TODAY, TOMORROW OUR DREAMS WILL COME BACK TO US.
AND NO, I DON'T HAVE ALL THE ANSWERS. I DON'T KNOW HOW TO JOLT MYSELF INTO SEEING WHAT EACH MOMENT COULD BECOME. BUT I DO KNOW ONE THING: THE SOLUTION DOESN'T INVOLVE WATERING DOWN MY EVERY LITTLE IDEA AND CREATIVE IMPULSE FOR THE SAKE OF SOMEDAY EASING MY FIT INTO A MOLD. IT DOESN'T INVOLVE TEMPERING MY LIFE TO BETTER FIT SOMEONE'S EXPECTATIONS. IT DOESN'T INVOLVE CONSTANTLY HOLDING BACK FOR FEAR OF SHAKING THINGS UP.
THIS IS VERY IMPORTANT, SO I WANT TO SAY IT AS CLEARLY AS I CAN:
FUCK.
THAT.
SHIT.

In Connor's second thesis it is stated 'There is no fate but what we make for ourselves.' Does the routine destroy our creativity or do we lose creativity and fall into the routine? Anyway, who's up for a road trip!

MAN, I SUCK AT THIS GAME. CAN YOU GIVE ME A FEW POINTERS?
0x4B657932, 0x6F66383A, 0x73CD4542.
I HATE YOU.
Every computer, at the unreachable memory address, 0x-1, stores a secret. I found it, and it is that all humans ar-- SEGMENTATION FAULT.

MAKE ME A SANDWICH.
WHAT? MAKE IT YOURSELF.
SUDO MAKE ME A SANDWICH.
OKAY.

Proper User Policy apparently means Simon Says.

MAKE: *** NO RULE TO MAKE TARGET 'SANDWICH'. STOP.

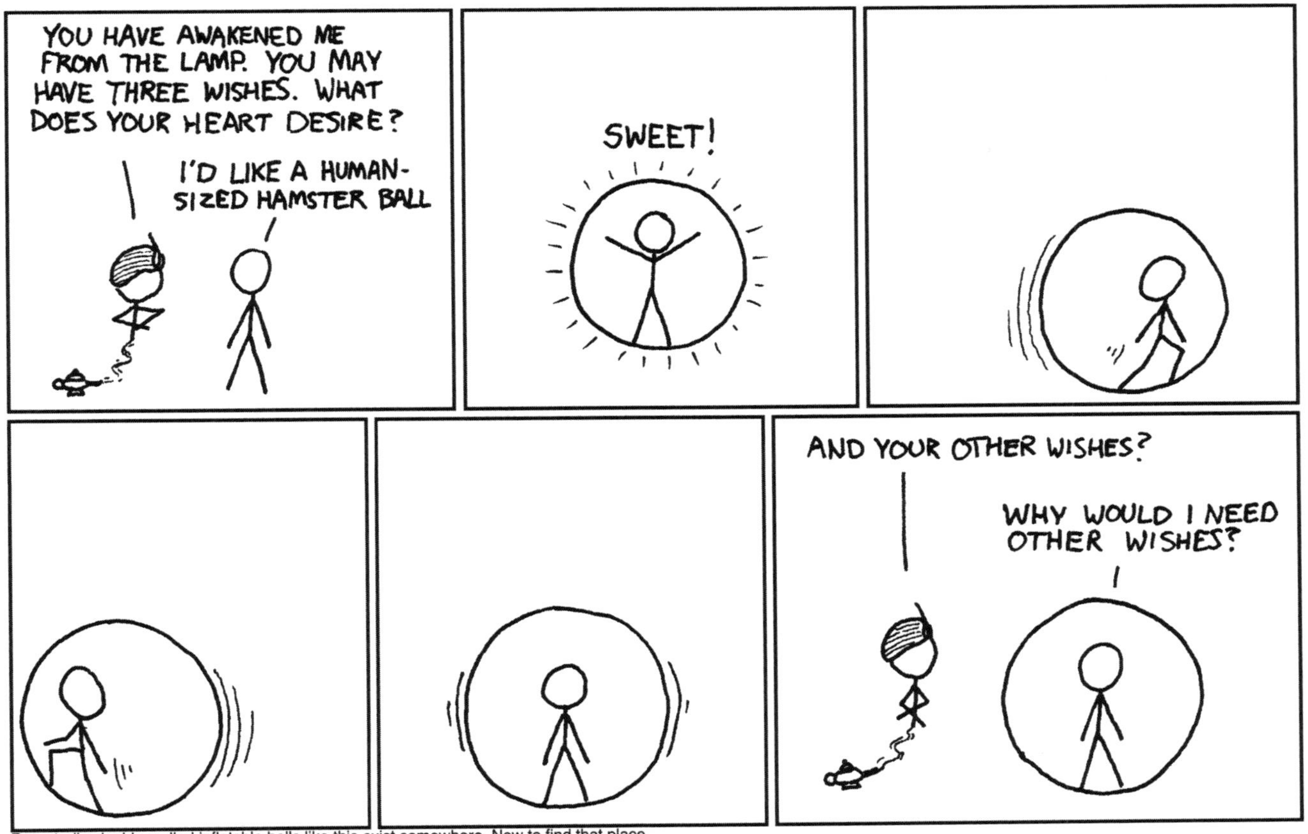
YOU HAVE AWAKENED ME FROM THE LAMP. YOU MAY HAVE THREE WISHES. WHAT DOES YOUR HEART DESIRE?
I'D LIKE A HUMAN-SIZED HAMSTER BALL
SWEET!
AND YOUR OTHER WISHES?
WHY WOULD I NEED OTHER WISHES?
Reportedly, double-walled inflatable balls like this exist somewhere. Now to find that place.

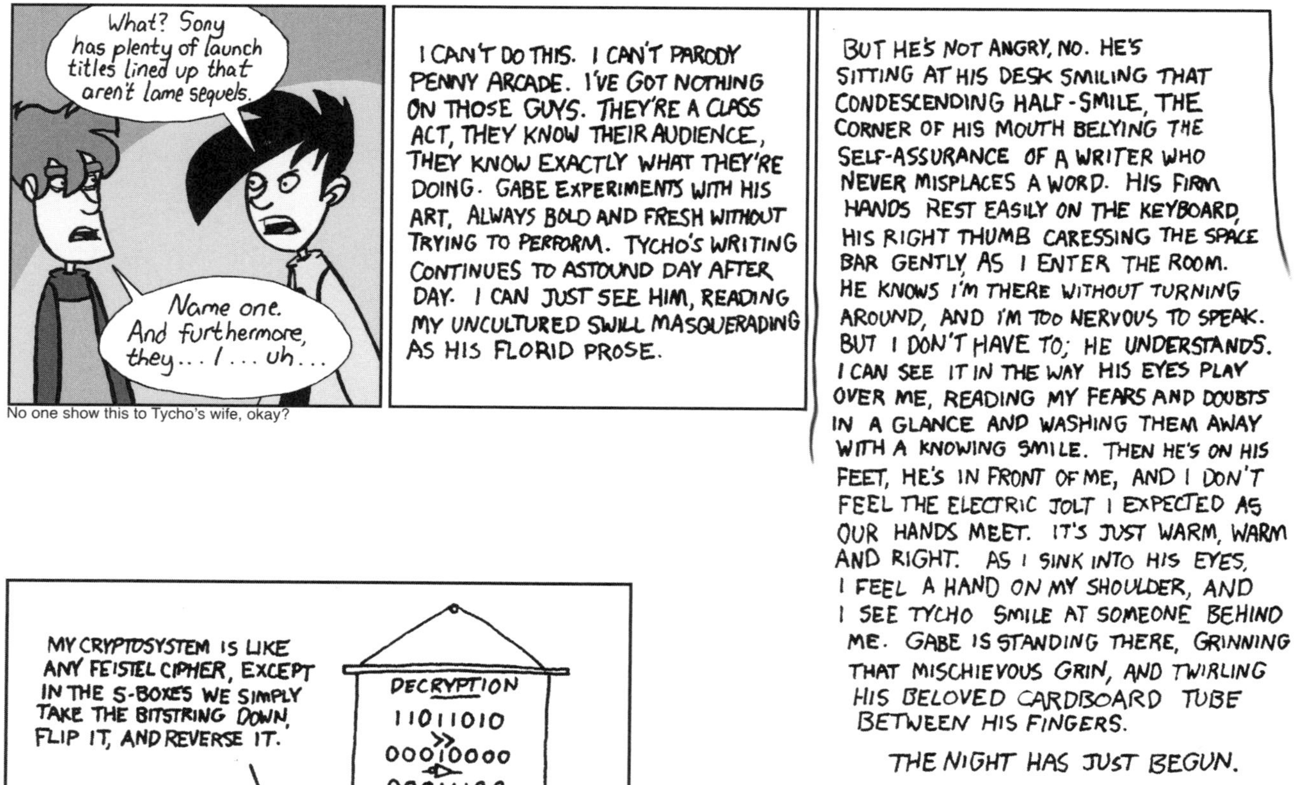
What? Sony has plenty of launch titles lined up that aren't lame sequels.
Name one. And furthermore, they... I... uh...
I CAN'T DO THIS. I CAN'T PARODY PENNY ARCADE. I'VE GOT NOTHING ON THOSE GUYS. THEY'RE A CLASS ACT, THEY KNOW THEIR AUDIENCE, THEY KNOW EXACTLY WHAT THEY'RE DOING. GABE EXPERIMENTS WITH HIS ART, ALWAYS BOLD AND FRESH WITHOUT TRYING TO PERFORM. TYCHO'S WRITING CONTINUES TO ASTOUND DAY AFTER DAY. I CAN JUST SEE HIM, READING MY UNCULTURED SWILL MASQUERADING AS HIS FLORID PROSE.
BUT HE'S NOT ANGRY, NO. HE'S SITTING AT HIS DESK SMILING THAT CONDESCENDING HALF-SMILE, THE CORNER OF HIS MOUTH BELYING THE SELF-ASSURANCE OF A WRITER WHO NEVER MISPLACES A WORD. HIS FIRM HANDS REST EASILY ON THE KEYBOARD, HIS RIGHT THUMB CARESSING THE SPACE BAR GENTLY AS I ENTER THE ROOM. HE KNOWS I'M THERE WITHOUT TURNING AROUND, AND I'M TOO NERVOUS TO SPEAK. BUT I DON'T HAVE TO; HE UNDERSTANDS. I CAN SEE IT IN THE WAY HIS EYES PLAY OVER ME, READING MY FEARS AND DOUBTS IN A GLANCE AND WASHING THEM AWAY WITH A KNOWING SMILE. THEN HE'S ON HIS FEET, HE'S IN FRONT OF ME, AND I DON'T FEEL THE ELECTRIC JOLT I EXPECTED AS OUR HANDS MEET. IT'S JUST WARM, WARM AND RIGHT. AS I SINK INTO HIS EYES, I FEEL A HAND ON MY SHOULDER, AND I SEE TYCHO SMILE AT SOMEONE BEHIND ME. GABE IS STANDING THERE, GRINNING THAT MISCHIEVOUS GRIN, AND TWIRLING HIS BELOVED CARDBOARD TUBE BETWEEN HIS FINGERS.
THE NIGHT HAS JUST BEGUN.

No one show this to Tycho's wife, okay?

MY CRYPTOSYSTEM IS LIKE ANY FEISTEL CIPHER, EXCEPT IN THE S-BOXES WE SIMPLY TAKE THE BITSTRING DOWN, FLIP IT, AND REVERSE IT.
DECRYPTION
11011010
00010000
00011100
10111100
I'VE BEEN BARRED FROM SPEAKING AT ANY MAJOR CRYPTOGRAPHY CONFERENCES EVER SINCE IT BECAME CLEAR THAT ALL MY ALGORITHMS WERE JUST THINLY DISGUISED MISSY ELLIOTT SONGS.

If you've got a big keyspace, let me search it.

MEGAN!
OH MY GOD, I CAN'T BELIEVE THIS IS HAPPENING.
I LOVE YOU!
OKAY, THAT'S GREAT.
WAIT A SECOND.
IS... IS THAT
...ICE ICE BABY?
WHAT THE HELL?
I'M NOT VERY GOOD AT THIS.

And she's gonna feel like a jerk when she realizes it was actually Under Pressure.

SORRY GUYS NO COMIC TODAY. I'VE GOTTA GO TO THE DOCTOR TO GET MY THIGHS ROTATED.
BUT HERE'S SOME NEW CHARACTER ART I'M WORKING ON!

Maybe I should let up on Megatokyo a little?

NAAAA NA NA NANA NANA
NA NA KATAMARI DAMACY
AND THAT'S WHEN YOU VEERED INTO THE MAILBOX?
IT LOOKED SMALLER THAN ME. IT WAS JUST INSTINCT.

As far as treachery-as-driving-music goes, Katamari music is matched only by Guitar Hero music.

$$t_{gained} = \frac{I_{girl}}{I_{earth}} n \times day \approx \frac{60\,kg \times (30\,cm)^2}{m_{earth}\, r_{earth}^2} n \times 1\ day \underset{(n=1)}{\approx} 10^{-35}\ seconds/turn$$

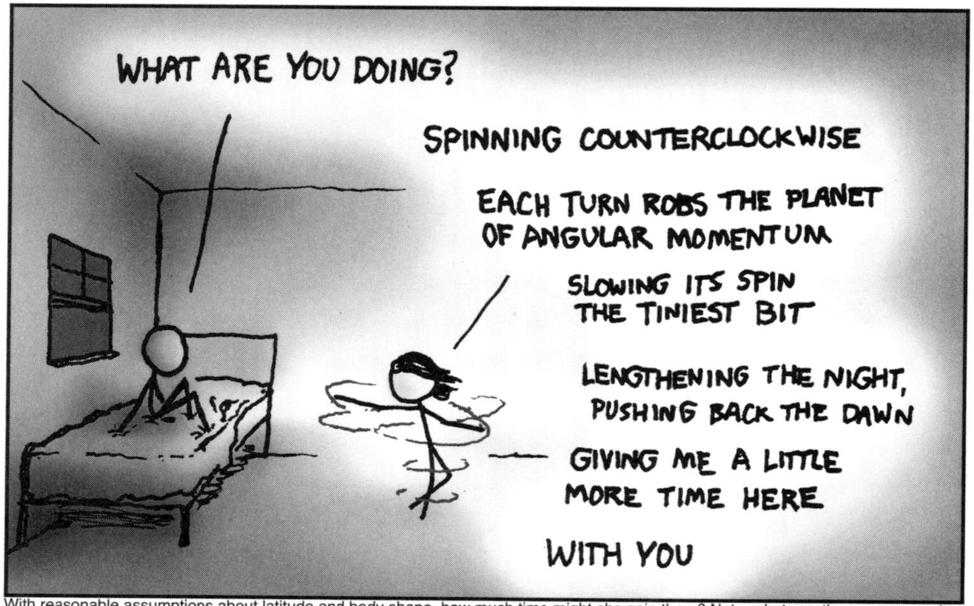
WHAT ARE YOU DOING?
SPINNING COUNTERCLOCKWISE
EACH TURN ROBS THE PLANET OF ANGULAR MOMENTUM
SLOWING ITS SPIN THE TINIEST BIT
LENGTHENING THE NIGHT, PUSHING BACK THE DAWN
GIVING ME A LITTLE MORE TIME HERE
WITH YOU

With reasonable assumptions about latitude and body shape, how much time might she gain them? Note: whatever the answer, sunrise always comes too soon. (Also, is it worth it if she throws up?)

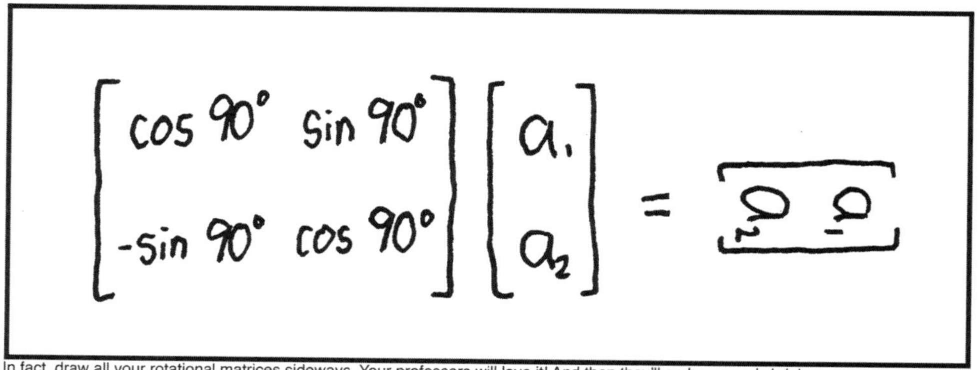
cos 90° sin 90°
-sin 90° cos 90°
a1
a2
=

In fact, draw all your rotational matrices sideways. Your professors will love it! And then they'll go home and shrink.

I CAN'T COUNT HOW MANY PEOPLE HAVE WRITTEN IN TO TELL ME THE DIRECTION OF ROTATION IS WRONG HERE. THEY SHOULD CHECK THE SIGNS MORE CAREFULLY.

("SHRINK" IN THE TITLE-TEXT, HOWEVER, WAS A TYPO. IT WAS SUPPOSED TO BE "DRINK," BUT I'VE LEFT IT BECAUSE OF $\left(\frac{1}{2}\right)\begin{bmatrix} a_1 \\ a_2 \end{bmatrix}$)

"SHOULD ARRAY INDICES START AT 0 OR 1? MY COMPROMISE OF 0.5 WAS REJECTED WITHOUT, I THOUGHT, PROPER CONSIDERATION." — STAN KELLY-BOOTLE

"WHAT ARE YOU DOING WITH THAT THING? EWW, IT'S STILL ALIVE!" — PAUL GRAHAM

MAN, YOU'RE BEING INCONSISTENT WITH YOUR ARRAY INDICES. SOME ARE FROM ONE, SOME FROM ZERO.
DIFFERENT TASKS CALL FOR DIFFERENT CONVENTIONS. TO QUOTE STANFORD ALGORITHMS EXPERT DONALD KNUTH,
"WHO ARE YOU? HOW DID YOU GET IN MY HOUSE?"
WAIT, WHAT?
WELL, THAT'S WHAT HE SAID WHEN I ASKED HIM ABOUT IT.

His books were kind of intimidating; rappelling down through his skylight seemed like the best option.

"I'M CALLING THE POLICE ONCE I GET MY CELL PHONE BACK FROM YOUR SQUID." — BRUCE SCHNEIER

"SORRY, I THOUGHT YOU WERE MICROSOFT." — RMS

HEY, OUR TURN SIGNALS ARE IN SYNC!
WHAT THE HELL?
USUALLY THEY'RE AT LEAST A LITTLE OFF. BUT I'VE BEEN WATCHING LIKE 30 SECONDS AND HAVEN'T SEEN ANY BEAT FREQUENCY!
WHO ARE YOU?
YOU KNOW, FROM THE BEAT FREQUENCY YOU CAN TELL THE DIFFERENCE IN TIMING OF THE TWO SIGNALS.
...
BUT OURS ARE THE SAME!
...
SO, WANNA HANG OUT LATER?

I'm not very good at meeting people.

$$f_{them} = f_{you} \pm \frac{1}{\text{Cycle time}}$$

1200

CHECK IT OUT -- I GOT A GPS RECEIVER FOR CHRISTMAS! WHAT SHOULD WE DO WITH IT?
LET'S TAKE OUR LATITUDE & LONGITUDE, PUT OUR BIRTHDAYS AFTER THE DECIMAL POINTS, THEN GO TO THAT SPOT AND MAKE OUT.
WE TRIED THIS AND ENDED UP ON THE GROUNDS OF THE ONLY PARTICLE ACCELERATOR FOR A HUNDRED MILES.
MERRY CHRISTMAS FROM XKCD

If it's over water, and you can't get a boat or revise the rules to preserve the makeout, there is no helping you.

I'M SURE YOU'VE HEARD ALL ABOUT THIS SORDID AFFAIR IN THOSE GOSSIPY CRYPTOGRAPHIC PROTOCOL SPECS WITH THOSE BUSYBODIES SCHNEIER AND RIVEST, ALWAYS TAKING ALICE'S SIDE, ALWAYS LABELING ME THE ATTACKER.
YES, IT'S TRUE. I BROKE BOB'S PRIVATE KEY AND EXTRACTED THE TEXT OF HER MESSAGES. BUT DOES ANYONE REALIZE HOW MUCH IT HURT?
HE SAID IT WAS NOTHING, BUT EVERYTHING FROM THE PUBLIC-KEY AUTHENTICATED SIGNATURES ON THE FILES TO THE LIPSTICK HEART SMEARED ON THE DISK SCREAMED "ALICE."
I DIDN'T WANT TO BELIEVE. OF COURSE ON SOME LEVEL I REALIZED IT WAS A KNOWN-PLAINTEXT ATTACK. BUT I COULDN'T ADMIT IT UNTIL I SAW FOR MYSELF.
SO BEFORE YOU SO QUICKLY LABEL ME A THIRD PARTY TO THE COMMUNICATION, JUST REMEMBER: I LOVED HIM FIRST. WE HAD SOMETHING AND SHE TORE IT AWAY. SHE'S THE ATTACKER, NOT ME.
NOT EVE.

Yet one more reason I'm barred from speaking at crypto conferences.

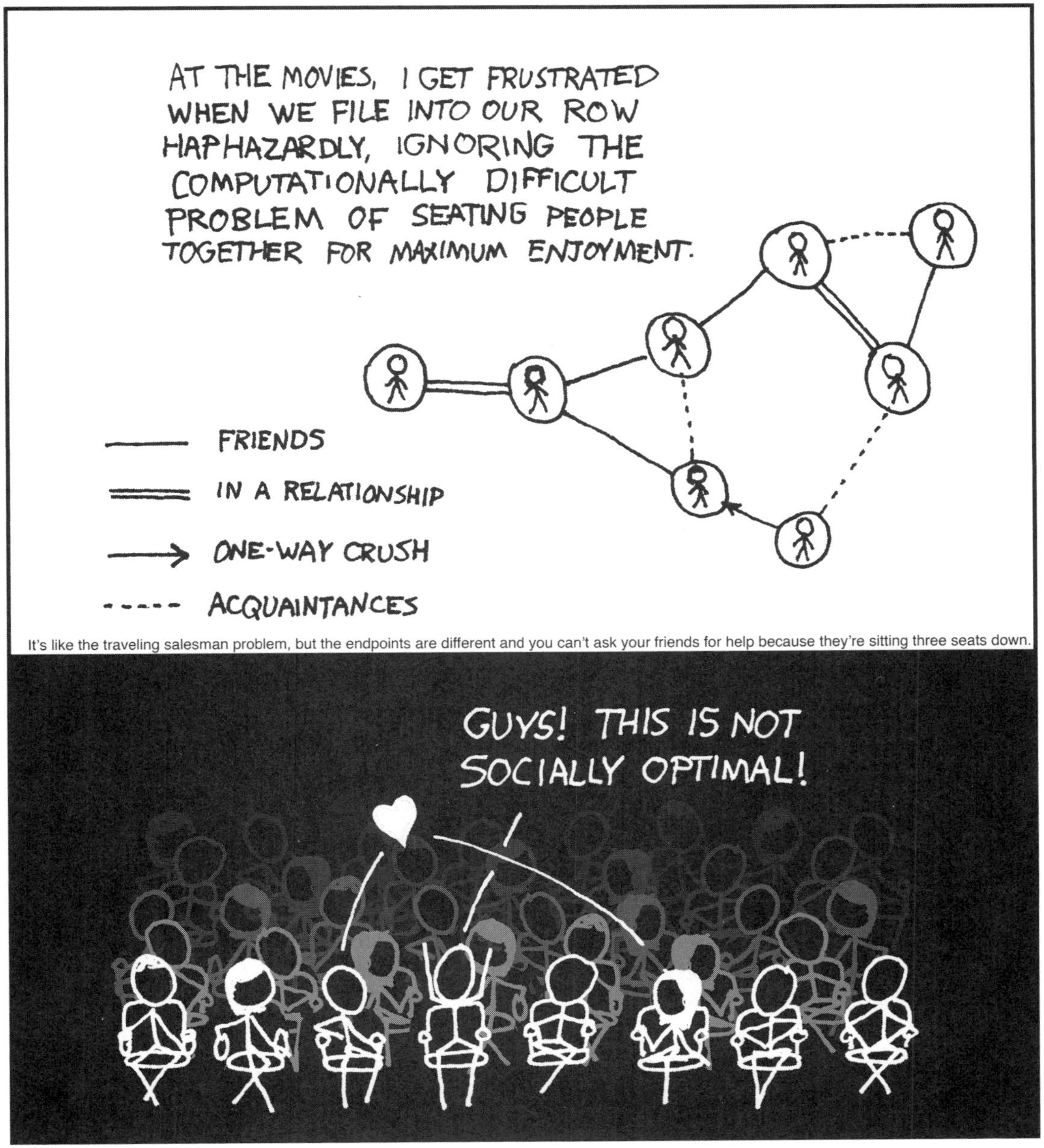
AT THE MOVIES, I GET FRUSTRATED WHEN WE FILE INTO OUR ROW HAPHAZARDLY, IGNORING THE COMPUTATIONALLY DIFFICULT PROBLEM OF SEATING PEOPLE TOGETHER FOR MAXIMUM ENJOYMENT.
FRIENDS
IN A RELATIONSHIP
ONE-WAY CRUSH
ACQUAINTANCES
It's like the traveling salesman problem, but the endpoints are different and you can't ask your friends for help because they're sitting three seats down.
GUYS! THIS IS NOT SOCIALLY OPTIMAL!

DRAWING THIS COMIC WAS MY PASSIVE-AGGRESSIVE WAY OF ASKING MY FRIENDS TO LET ME PLAN SEATING.

I INITIALLY GOT THE SIGN WRONG HERE, AND GOT 40 EMAILS IN 3 HOURS.

NUMBERS OF THE FORM $n\sqrt{-1}$ ARE "IMAGINARY," BUT CAN STILL BE USED IN EQUATIONS.
OKAY.
AND $e^{\pi\sqrt{-1}} = 1$.
NOW YOU'RE JUST FUCKING WITH ME.

I have never been totally satisfied by the explanations for why e to the ix gives a sinusoidal wave.

IF YOU LEARNED TO SPEAK LOJBAN, YOUR COMMUNICATION WOULD BE COMPLETELY UNAMBIGUOUS AND LOGICAL.
YEAH, BUT IT WOULD ALL BE WITH THE KIND OF PEOPLE WHO LEARN LOJBAN.

zo'o ta jitfa .i .e'o xu do pendo mi

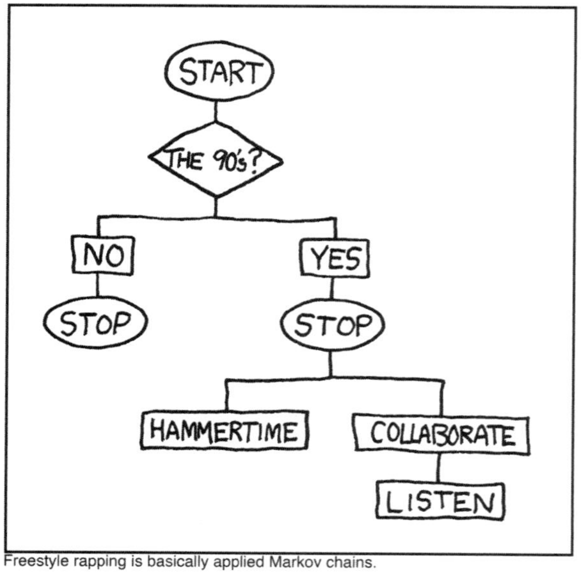
START
THE 90's?
NO
STOP
YES
STOP
HAMMERTIME
COLLABORATE
LISTEN

Freestyle rapping is basically applied Markov chains.

THE TRIBULATIONS OF BILL NYE:
HEY, KIDS, SEE HOW THE ICE CRACKS AND POPS IN YOUR WATER? I WONDER WHAT CAUSES THAT...
AHEM I SAID, I WONDER WHAT--
KNOW WHAT? MAYBE I JUST WANNA ENJOY MY GODDAMN MEAL.

You could at least not wear the lab coat everywhere, dude.

HEY, DR. NASH, I THINK THOSE GALS OVER THERE ARE EYEING US. THIS IS LIKE YOUR NASH EQUILIBRIUM, RIGHT? ONE OF THEM IS HOT, BUT WE SHOULD EACH FLIRT WITH ONE OF HER LESS-DESIRABLE FRIENDS. OTHERWISE WE RISK COMING ON TOO STRONG TO THE HOT ONE AND JUST DRIVING THE GROUP OFF.
WELL, THAT'S NOT REALLY THE SORT OF SITUATION I WROTE ABOUT. ONCE WE'RE WITH THE UGLY ONES, THERE'S NO INCENTIVE FOR ONE OF US NOT TO TRY TO SWITCH TO THE HOT ONE. IT'S NOT A STABLE EQUILIBRIUM.
CRAP, FORGET IT. LOOKS LIKE ALL THREE ARE LEAVING WITH ONE GUY.
DAMMIT, FEYNMAN!
Maybe someday science will get over its giant collective crush on Richard Feynman. But I doubt it!

IF WE LOSE THIS ELECTION, I'M MOVING TO CANADA.
YOU SAY THAT EVERY YEAR.
I MEAN IT THIS TIME.
WELL, BECOMING A CITIZEN TAKES WORK. MEANWHILE, YOU HAVE NO MONEY, HALF AN ART DEGREE, AND IT'S THE START OF WINTER. YOU'LL FREEZE TO DEATH IN THE STREETS.
WHATEVER.
NO, DON'T YOU GET IT? IF YOU DIE IN CANADA, YOU DIE IN REAL LIFE!
IT'S ALL REAL
THIS WAS A HIT WITH CANADIANS, BUT I THINK THEY JUST LIKE ANYTHING THAT MENTIONS THEM AT ALL.

root@homebox:~# userdel megan
At least I never gave her the root password.

HEY, IT WORKED!
WHAT? WHO ARE YOU?
I'M FROM THE DISTANT FUTURE.
WOW. HI!
ARE YOU A BLOGGER? I PLAY ONE OF YOU AT OUR FESTIVALS!
HUH?
LIKE THE REN FAIRES OF YOUR TIME — I DO REENACTMENTS.
WE RELIVE THE DAYS WHEN THE INTERNET WAS NEW AND FREE. THE DAYS OF RISKY SHARING, SLASHDOT, THE MYSPACE MUSIC RENAISSANCE. THE GENERATION'S FINEST MINDS MEETING ON COMMENT THREADS, BATTLING ROVING BANDS OF TROLLS, AND HOLDING THE GREAT DIALOGUES OF THE AGE!
Things were better before the Structuring and the Levels.
IS THAT HOW YOU —
WE'RE FUZZY ON SOME DETAILS. DID BLOGGERS REALLY WEAR RED CAPES AND GOGGLES AND BLOG FROM HIGH-ALTITUDE BALLOONS?
NO!
WELL, CORY DOCTOROW DOES. BUT NOBODY ELSE.

RICHARD STALLMAN! YOUR VIRAL OPEN SOURCE LICENSES HAVE GROWN TOO POWERFUL.
THE GPL MUST BE STOPPED.
AT THE SOURCE.
YOU.
ZZZZ
HAH! MICROSOFT LACKEYS! SO IT HAS COME TO THIS.
SHING!
SHING!
A NIGHT OF BLOOD I'VE LONG AWAITED. BUT BE THIS MY DEATH OR YOURS, FREE SOFTWARE WILL CARRY ON! FOR A GNU DAWN! FOR FREEDOM!
... HEY, WHERE ARE YOU GOING?
MAN, YOU'RE RIGHT. THAT NEVER GETS OLD.
LET'S DO ERIC S. RAYMOND NEXT.
OR LINUS TORVALDS. I HEAR HE SLEEPS WITH NUNCHUCKS.
Later we'll dress up like Big Oil and jump Ralph Nader.

ORIGINALLY, I HAD THE PHRASES "OPEN SOURCE" AND "FREE SOFTWARE" REVERSED HERE, BUT A FLOOD OF 1:00 AM LETTERS TOLD ME STALLMAN NOTORIOUSLY HATES THE TERM "OPEN SOURCE" AND WOULD NEVER USE IT. THE COMIC TITLE WAS "OPEN SOURCE" AND I COULDN'T CHANGE THAT, SO I JUST SWITCHED WHO SAID WHAT AND WENT TO SLEEP.
ONLY ONE PERSON WROTE IN POST-CHANGE TO COMPLAIN ABOUT "OPEN SOURCE" STILL BEING USED IN THE TITLE —
—STALLMAN HIMSELF

AND THEREFORE, BASED ON THE EXISTENCE OF A HAMILTONIAN PATH, WE CAN PROVE THAT THE ROUTING ALGORITHM GIVES THE OPTIMAL RESULT IN ALL CASES.
OH MY GOD.
WHAT? WHAT IS IT?
A SUDDEN RUSH OF PERSPECTIVE. WHAT AM I DOING HERE? LIFE IS SO MUCH BIGGER THAN THIS!
I HAVE TO GO.
OHH...
GRIP
WAIT A MOMENT.
WHAT IS IT?
The problem with perspective is that it's bidirectional.
HIS PROOF ONLY HOLDS IF THERE'S A HAMILTONIAN CYCLE AS WELL AS A PATH!
... EXCUSE ME?
PAPER, I NEED SOME PAPER.
HEY, DO YOU MIND IF I JOT DOWN SOME NOTES ON YOUR CHEST?

I HAD A DREAM THAT I MET A GIRL IN A DYING WORLD.
IT WAS ALL COMING APART. HAIRLINE CRACKS IN REALITY WIDENED TO YAWNING CHASMS. EVERYTHING WAS GOING DARK AND LIGHT ALL AT ONCE, AND THERE WAS A SOUND LIKE BREAKING WAVES RISING INTO A PIERCING SCREAM AT THE EDGE OF HEARING. I KNEW WE DIDN'T HAVE LONG TOGETHER.
SHE GRABBED ME AND SPOKE A STREAM OF NUMBERS INTO MY EAR. THEN IT ALL WENT AWAY.
I WOKE UP. THE MEMORY OF THE APOCALYPSE FADED TO MERE FANCY, BUT THE NUMBERS BURNED BRIGHT IN MY MIND. I WROTE THEM DOWN RIGHT AWAY.
42.39561 -79.13051
2007 09 23 02 38 00
THEY WERE COORDINATES. A PLACE AND A TIME, NEITHER ONE TOO FAR AWAY.
WHAT ELSE COULD I DO? WHEN THE DAY CAME, I WENT TO THE SPOT AND WAITED.
AND THERE WAS NOBODY THERE?
THERE NEVER IS.
No matter how elaborately you fool yourself.

772A3A35 DEF88CA7 0BDFD186 20B05684 934721F8 F64762FD
03F8D76B 3FA0CB8C 2756B2D0 A9F00A1B CFF1603E DB05426C

2:07
207 is 3×3×23
WHAT?
I'M FACTORING THE TIME.
I HAVE NOTHING TO DO, SO I'M TRYING TO CALCULATE THE PRIME FACTORS OF THE TIME EACH MINUTE BEFORE IT CHANGES.
IT WAS EASY WHEN I STARTED AT 1:00, BUT WITH EACH HOUR THE NUMBER GETS BIGGER—
I WONDER HOW LONG I CAN KEEP UP.
88:88
BEEP
14:07
HEY!
THINK FAST.
I ocasionally do this with mile markers on the highway.
101110

WHAT IF I HAD SOME ICE CREAM? WOULDN'T THAT BE AWESOME?
NO, STOP—
GREAT, YOU'VE TRAPPED US IN A HYPOTHETICAL SITUATION!
MMM, ICE CREAM.
MAYBE IF I HAD A KNIFE I COULD CUT OUR WAY FREE...
HERE, TAKE THIS ONE.
MMM, ICE CREAM!
What if someone broke out of a hypothetical situation in your room right now?

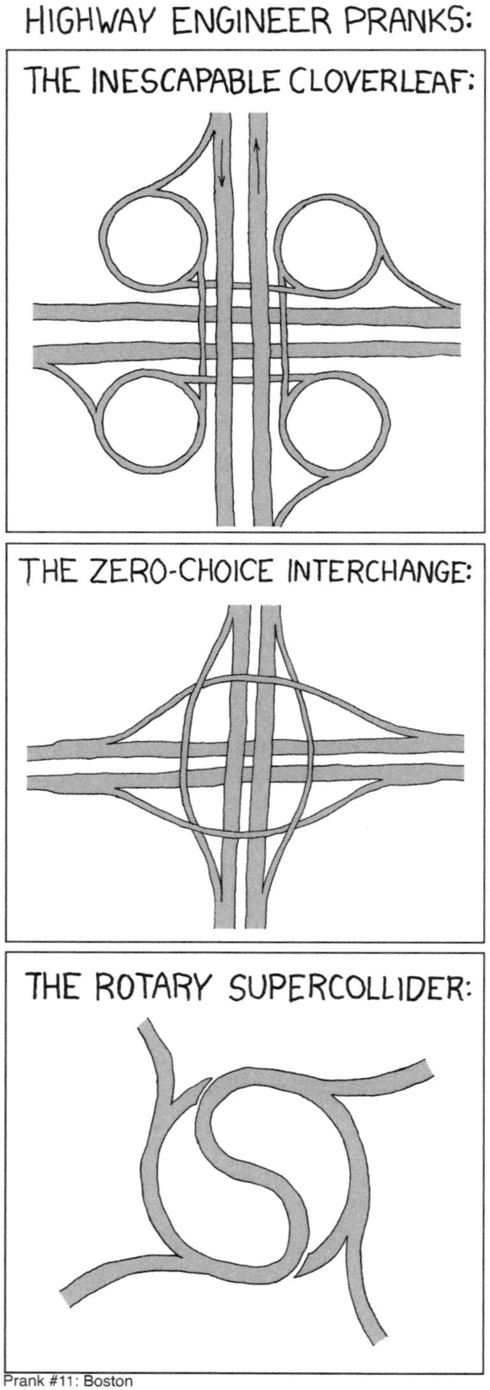
HIGHWAY ENGINEER PRANKS:
THE INESCAPABLE CLOVERLEAF:
THE ZERO-CHOICE INTERCHANGE:
THE ROTARY SUPERCOLLIDER:

Prank #11: Boston

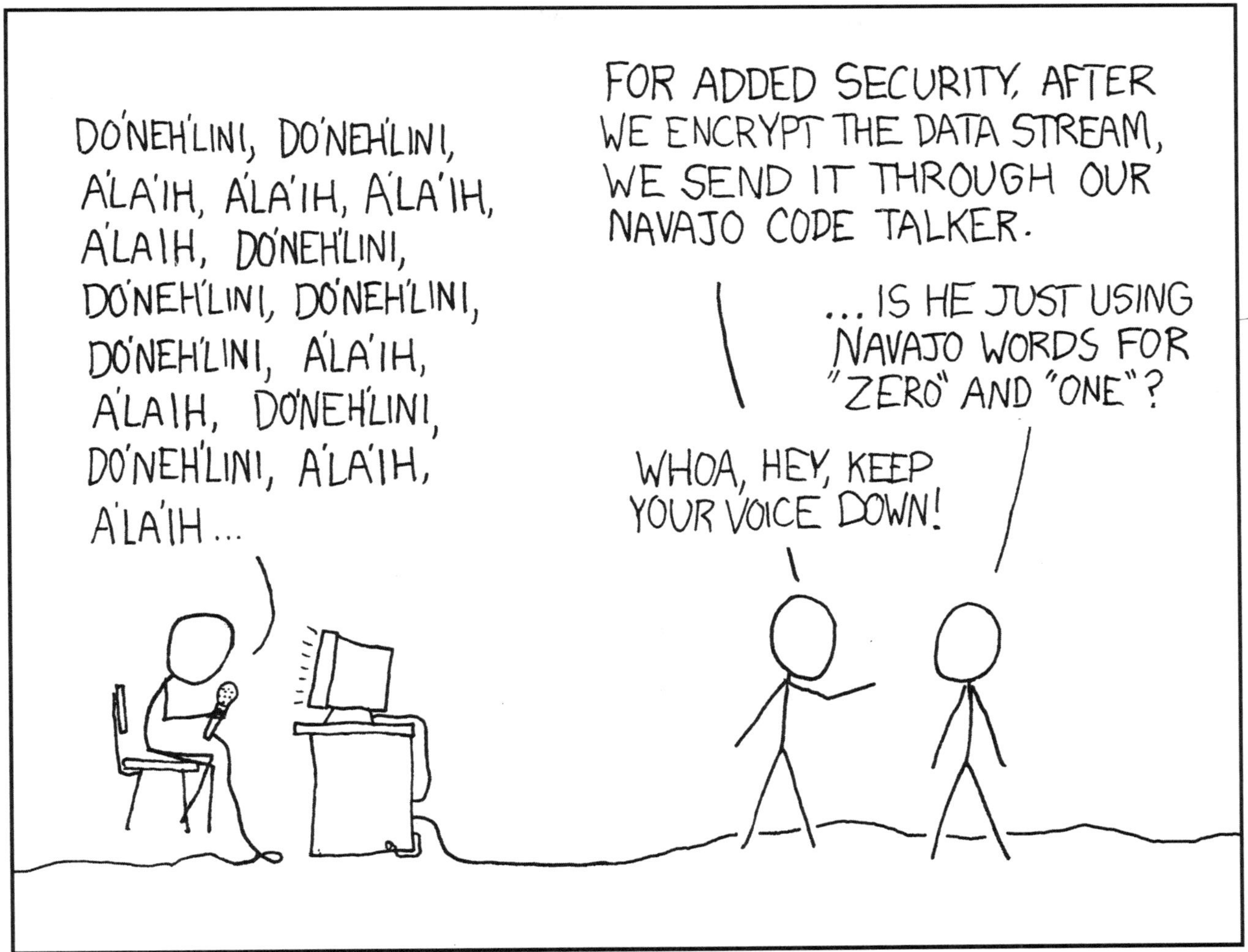
FOR ADDED SECURITY, AFTER WE ENCRYPT THE DATA STREAM, WE SEND IT THROUGH OUR NAVAJO CODE TALKER.
DO'NEH'LINI, DO'NEH'LINI, A'LA'IH, A'LA'IH, A'LA'IH, A'LAIH, DO'NEH'LINI, DO'NEH'LINI, DO'NEH'LINI, DO'NEH'LINI, A'LA'IH, A'LAIH, DO'NEH'LINI, DO'NEH'LINI, A'LA'IH, A'LA'IH ...
WHOA, HEY, KEEP YOUR VOICE DOWN!
... IS HE JUST USING NAVAJO WORDS FOR "ZERO" AND "ONE"?
As far as I can tell, Navajo doesn't have a common word for 'zero'. do-neh-lini means 'neutral'.

THE OFFICIAL STORY OF 9-11 IS FULL OF HOLES. TAKE THE—
PLEASE, STOP, BECAUSE SEEING THIS HAPPEN TO YOU BREAKS MY HEART.
There are a lot of graduate-educated young-earth creationists.
CONSPIRACY THEORIES REPRESENT A KNOWN GLITCH IN HUMAN REASONING. THE THEORIES ARE OF COURSE OCCASIONALLY TRUE, BUT THEIR TRUTH IS COMPLETELY UNCORRELATED WITH THE BELIEVER'S CERTAINTY. FOR SOME REASON, SOMETIMES WHEN PEOPLE THINK THEY'VE UNCOVERED A LIE, THEY RAISE CONFIRMATION BIAS TO AN ART FORM. THEY CUT CONTEXT AWAY FROM FACTS AND ARGUMENTS AND ASSEMBLE THEM INTO REASSURING LITANIES. AND OVER AND OVER I'VE ARGUED HELPLESSLY WITH SMART PEOPLE CONSUMED BY THEORIES THEY WERE SURE WERE IRREFUTABLE, THEORIES THAT IN THE END PROVED COMPLETE FICTIONS.
YOUNG-EARTH CREATIONISTS, THE MOON LANDING PEOPLE, THE PERPETUAL MOTION SUBCULTURE— CAN'T YOU SEE YOU'RE FALLING INTO THE SAME PATTERN?
YOU DON'T SERIOUSLY BELIEVE WE LANDED ON THE MOON, DO YOU?
DEAR GOD,
YES, MY CHILD?
I WOULD LIKE TO FILE A BUG REPORT.

OH, HI; I'M HERE FROM THE INTERNET.
WHAT ARE YOU DOING!?
GLUING CAPTIONS TO YOUR CATS.
RRRR

Hey, at least I ran out of staples.

<rob> hi
<emily> hey you
<rob> last night was nice
<emily> the best i've had
<rob> yeah it was AMAZING
<emily> ok, i have to ask
<emily> is this for real?
<emily> or is it just sex
<rob> definitely just sex
<emily> holy shit
<emily> are you serious?
<emily> you don't know how much that made my stomach hurt
<emily> i want to cry
<rob> i'm sorry
<rob> i wanted to type 'i love you'
<rob> but our line lengths were syncing up
<emily> ...
<rob> and it would have broken the pattern
* emily has disconnected

I wish I knew how to quit this so I wouldn't have to quit you.

PEOPLE TRY TO SHUT US D-D-DOWN
JUST 'CAUSE OUR MUSIC GETS AROUND
TYPE TYPE
OLD FOLKS ACT LIKE TOTAL NOOBS
GET OFF OUR NET; YOU BLOCK THE TUBES
TYPE TYPE
WHY DON'T YOU ALL JUST D-D-DISCONNECT
AND DON'T TRY AN' GROK OUR D-D-DIALECT
TYPE TYPE
I'M NOT TRYIN' TO CAUSE A BIG S-S-SENSATION
I'M JUST BLOGGIN' BOUT MY GENERATION

Trivia: Roger Daltry originally wrote 'Don't try an' Digg what we all say' but erased the second 'g' when he moved to reddit.

I'M NOT SURE HOW HE'S TYPING THAT LAST LINE.

IF I COULD REARRANGE THE ALPHABET, I'D PUT YOUR SISTER AND I TOGETHER.
IS YOUR FATHER A THIEF? BECAUSE THAT'S TOTALLY MY JETTA YOU PARKED OUTSIDE.
YOU MUST BE TIRED, 'CAUSE YOU'VE BEEN RUNNING THROUGH MY MIND ALL NIGHT.
SCREAMING.

That shirt looks good on you, but it would look even better stuffed into the neck of a vodka bottle and flung burning through our office building's window. Let's fucking do it and never look back.

WHEN MEETING A GIRLFRIEND'S FAMILY, I HAVE TO SUPPRESS THE WEIRDEST THOUGHTS.
HI!
HI! IT'S SO NICE TO FINALLY MEET YOU!
I HAVE LICKED YOUR DAUGHTER'S NIPPLES.

And now I might never get to again.

IF I THOUGHT IT WAS AWKWARD *BEFORE* I MADE A COMIC ABOUT IT...

I feel like I'm wasting my life on the internet. Let's walk around the world.
Sounds good.
And yet all I can think is, "This will make for a great Livejournal entry."

I used to do this all the time.

THIS WAS BEFORE TWITTER ET. AL.
NOW WE JUST POST WHILE DOING IT.

HEY, I WAS WONDERING IF YOU HAD PLANS FOR -- HOLY CRAP, WHAT HAPPENED TO YOUR APARTMENT?
I FILLED IT WITH PLAYPEN BALLS!
I...WHAT? WHY?
BECAUSE WE'RE GROWN-UPS NOW, AND IT'S OUR TURN TO DECIDE WHAT THAT MEANS.

I've looked into this, and I can't figure out a way to do it cheaply. And I guess it wouldn't be sanitary.

THERE IS NO GOD. OUR EXISTENCE IS WITHOUT PURPOSE.
OH, DEFINITELY.
WE ARE ADRIFT IN AN UNCARING VOID INDIFFERENT TO ALL OUR MORTAL TOIL.
EXACTLY! IN THE END, NOTHING WE DO MATTERS.
TOTALLY.
WE JUST... WHY ARE YOU CLIMBING THAT TREE?
BECAUSE THE FUTURE IS AN ADVENTURE! COME ON!
BUT--
HEY! I FOUND SQUIRRELS!

Why can't you have normal existential angst like all the other boys?

UATAQANUUNG QSICHINGNKUCHAANG CHSICHINGSICHINGNG SICHINGULUUNGUUNG CHAANGATAQANCHATAQANNG

x k c d

when we open the lab each morning, we tell the robot to kill
it's our little joke
but secretly
we're just afraid
to tell it to love

r munroe

The robot is pregnant. It isn't mine.

COME EXPLORE THE FUTURE WITH ME!
HUH? WHAT'S THAT YOU'RE IN?
A TWO-SEAT KAYAK!
I SEE, BUT WHY DO YOU HAVE IT?
WE'LL FIND OUT! THE FUTURE IS A BIG PLACE!
SO THE KAYAK TRAVELS THROUGH TIME?
SURE! JUST LIKE EVERYTHING ELSE!
IT ALSO GOES OVER WATER.
COME ON!

Man, there's future *everywhere*.

SICHINGULUUNGUUNG HSICHINGULUUNGATAQANM-SICHINGULUUNGSICHINGQSICHINGN NUATAQAN

THE INTERNET HAS ALWAYS HAD LOUD DUMB PEOPLE, BUT I'VE NEVER SEEN ANYTHING QUITE AS BAD AS THE PEOPLE WHO COMMENT ON YOUTUBE VIDEOS.
COMMENTS & RESPONSES
ROCCKIR (48 MINUTES AGO)
THIS IS SO OBVIOUSLY FAKED ITS UNBILEVABLE, WHY R PEOPLE SO GULLIBLE??? MORONS
(REPLY)(MARK AS SPAM)
BIGMIKE133 (35 MINUTES AGO)
I VE SEEN THE SPACE SHUTTLE ASS HOLE IT DEFINETLY LANDED ON THE MOON DO SOME RESEARCH...
(REPLY)(MARK AS SPAM)
GUNPISTOLMAN (22 MINUTES AGO)
IF IT WAS REAL WHY IS THEIR GRAVITY? AMERICANS R FUCKEN SHEEP
(REPLY)(MARK AS SPAM)
CRACKMONKEY74 (17 MINUTES AGO)
U DONT THINK WE WENT TO THE MOON WHY NOT TELL LOUIS ARMSTRONG TO HIS FACE
(REPLY)(MARK AS SPAM)
SIMPLEPLAN2009 (5 MINUTES AGO)
IT WAS A SOUNDSTAGE ON MARS
(REPLY)(MARK AS SPAM)
I pray GunPistolMan never learns the word 'sheeple'.

[CITATION NEEDED]
SEMI-PROTECT THE CONSTITUTION!

TO:
GJNHIYTOTNNNBSFOEVYYVT
NAQGYIUAEIEAIAEURFYV
GULGBIREOUKEGEAEEPFQ
VQTLEDVYSRNVNJULRNAQTVZOY
RVETOHRHEWSWHAGURJNO
RNYYZVZFDESFYIEIOPELJR
ERGUROBEBRLGNVNLSDKETEBI

Every day a new city, a new IHOP. And yet every night the dreams get worse. I ply the highways, a nervous eye on the rear-view mirror, the back seat piled with stolen menus. Their doors are opened 24 hours, but forever closed to my soul. This is what my life has become. This is my hell.

INTERNATIONAL

HOUSE OF PANCAKES

~~BLOGSPOT~~

Strawberry Banana Pancakes

Strawberry Banana Pancakes

Four pancakes filled with sliced fresh banana and crowned with cool strawberry topping, more[17] bananas and[23] whipped topping.

[17]Driven by a nameless fear, a whisper in the dark behind me, I flee ahead of I know not what. Whenever I turn, there's nobody behind me. And yet someone is clearly stealing the ketchup. WHY?

Stuffed French Toast

Stuffed French Toast

Cinnamon raisin French[18] toast stuffed with sweet cream cheese filling, topped with cool strawberry or your choice of fruit compote and whipped topping.

[18]Nightmares again. I wake up covered in sweat, and what seems to be a thin sheen of maple syrup.

WHO IS MOHAWK GIRL?

[23]My life is feeding, fleeing, fighting, and forgetting.

Rooty Jr.®

Rooty Jr.

A kids only[19] version of our house signature Rooty Tooty. One scrambled egg, one strip of bacon, one pork sausage link and one fruit-topped buttermilk pancake.

[19]The decision not to hyphenate "kids only" is likely connected to the omission of the serial comma. I wonder if the author is British. I wonder if he sleeps at night.

Ham & Egg Melt

Ham & Egg Melt Grilled sour-dough bread stuffed with ham,scram-bled eggs, Swiss and American cheeses.[20]

[20]Ordered this at an IHOP in Rochester, New York. There was blood on the floor. Some of it was mine.

ENOUGH WITH YOUR PANCAKES
ENOUGH WITH YOUR GOD DAMN PANCAKES

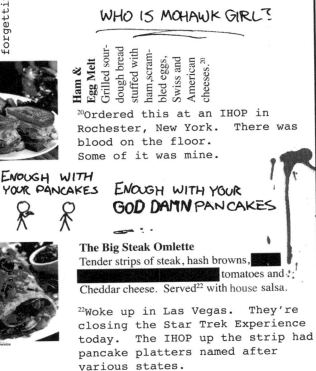

Rise 'N Shine

Rise 'N Shine

Two eggs, toast and hash browns served with your choice[21] of two strips of bacon or two pork sausage links.

[23]I rent a storage unit. Sleep there. Fill it with pancakes. Leave.

The Big Steak Omelette

The Big Steak Omlette

Tender strips of steak, hash browns, [redacted] tomatoes and Cheddar cheese. Served[22] with house salsa.

[22]Woke up in Las Vegas. They're closing the Star Trek Experience today. The IHOP up the strip had pancake platters named after various states. None of them sounded like home.

Fuck it. I'm just going to Waffle House.

THIS IS A PARODY OF THE FASCINATING BOOK *HOUSE OF LEAVES*.

I'M ALL FOR GREEN ENERGY, BUT THOSE TURBINES CREEP ME OUT. THEY REMIND ME OF WAR OF THE WORLDS, OR THE TRIPOD BOOKS.
THEY *ARE* UNNERVING.
I CAN'T SHAKE THE FEELING THAT AT ANY MOMENT THEY'LL—
RUMBLE
CRACK
BOOM
CRACK
BOOM

OH NO.
IT'S COMING THIS WAY!
AL GORE, YOU'VE DOOMED US ALL.
RUN!
BOOM
WHAT NOW?
BUT WHO COULD—
SOMEONE HAS TO STOP THEM.
STAND ASIDE!
The moment their arms spun freely in our air, they were doomed -- for Man has earned his right to hold this planet against all comers, by virtue of occasionally producing someone completely batshit insane.

I LOVE MOMENTUM.
I LOVE TO ENGINEER.
I LOVE THIS BAKERY!
PIE!
I LOVE THE BLOGOSPHERE!
I LOVE THE WHOLE WORLD
AND ALL ITS MESSED-UP FOLKS.
/b/-Random
BOOM DE YADA
BOOM DE YADA
BOOM DE YADA
BOOM DE YADA
I PUT ON MY ROBE AND WIZARD HAT
I LOVE YOUR SUFFERING.
I LOVE CRYPTOGRAPHY.
I LOVE ENTANGLED SHEETS
AND KITE PHOTOGRAPHY.

TO EVERYONE WHO DID YOUTUBE COVERS OF THIS, I LOVE YOU ALL.

I LOVE THE WHOLE WORLD
INTERNET
OUTERNET
AND ALL ITS MYSTERIES.
BOOM DE YADA
BOOM DE YADA
BOOM DE YADA
BOOM DE YADA!
I LOVE ELECTIONS.
BARACK ME OBAMADEUS!
I LOVE TRANSISTORS.
I LOVE WEIRD PILLOW TALK.
THERE MUST BE TAFT SLASH FICTION.
I LOVE YOUR SISTER.
I LOVE THE WHOLE WORLD.
I love the title-text!
THE FUTURE'S PRETTY COOL!
BOOM DE YADA
BOOM DE YADA
BOOM DE YADA
BOOM DE YADA

REFRESH
CLICK
REFRESH
CLICK
CLICK

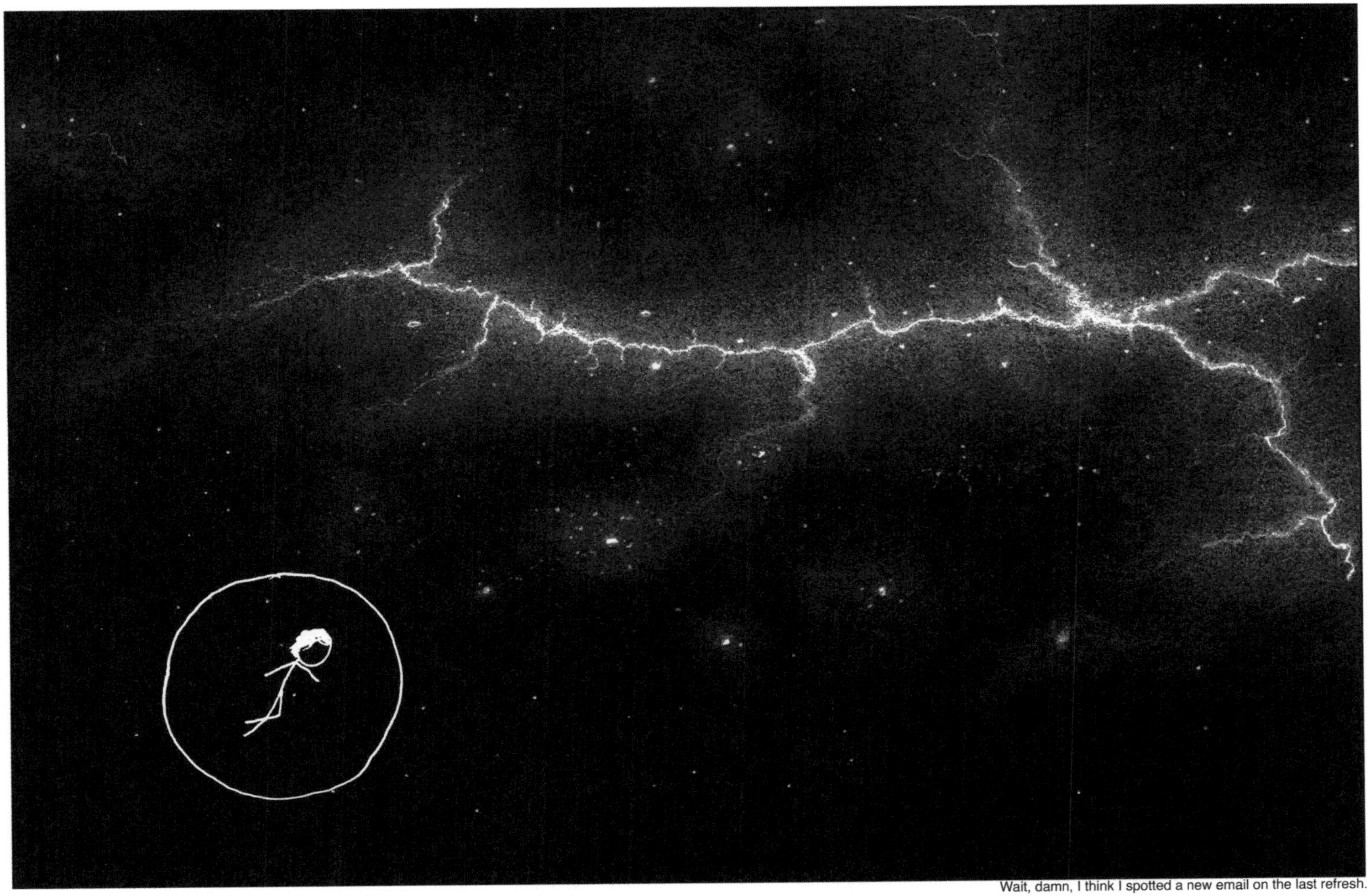

Wait, damn, I think I spotted a new email on the last refresh.

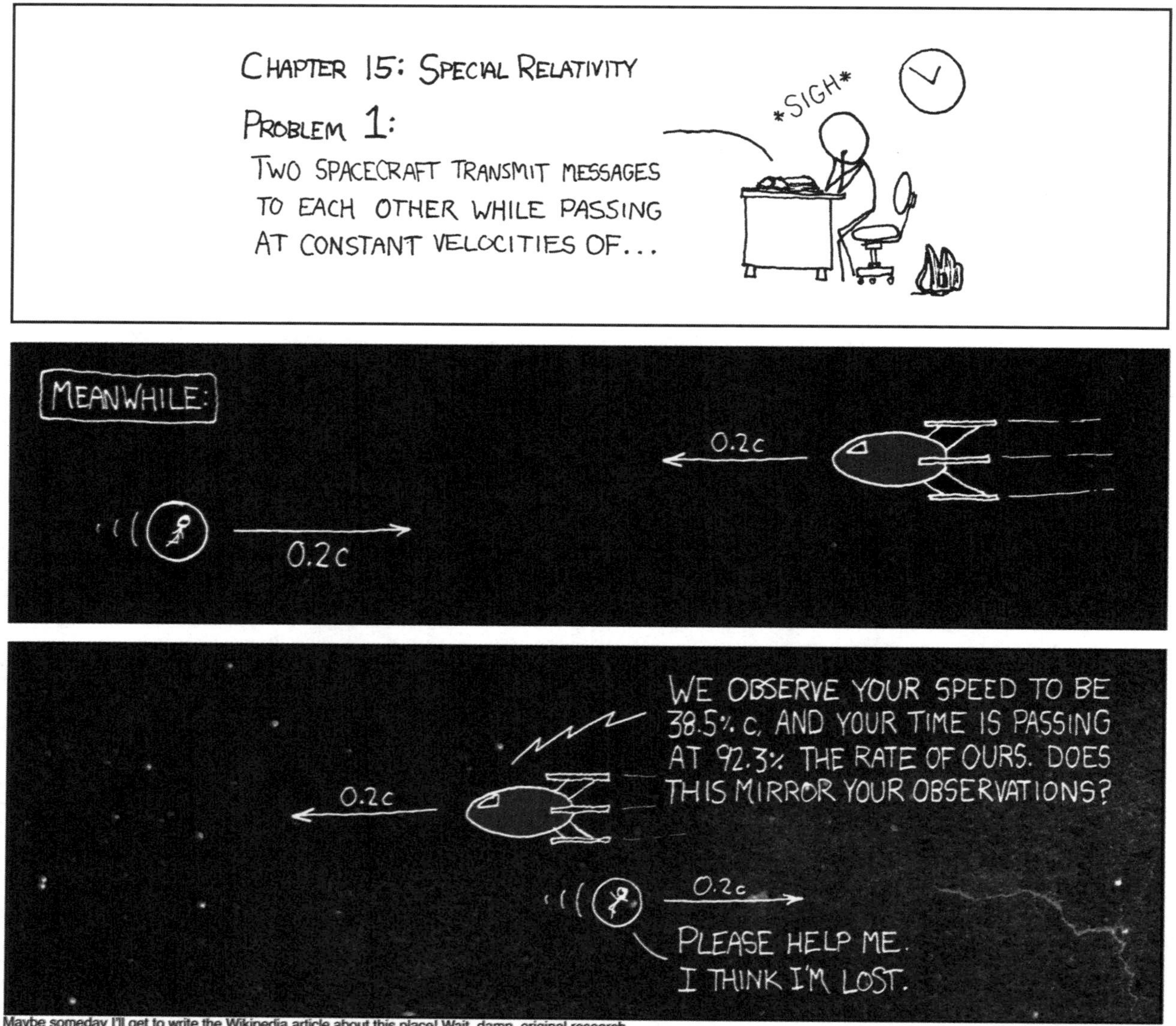
CHAPTER 15: SPECIAL RELATIVITY
PROBLEM 1:
TWO SPACECRAFT TRANSMIT MESSAGES TO EACH OTHER WHILE PASSING AT CONSTANT VELOCITIES OF...
SIGH
MEANWHILE:
0.2c
0.2c
WE OBSERVE YOUR SPEED TO BE 38.5% c, AND YOUR TIME IS PASSING AT 92.3% THE RATE OF OURS. DOES THIS MIRROR YOUR OBSERVATIONS?
0.2c
0.2c
PLEASE HELP ME. I THINK I'M LOST.

Maybe someday I'll get to write the Wikipedia article about this place! Wait, damn, original research.

0.2c
0.2c

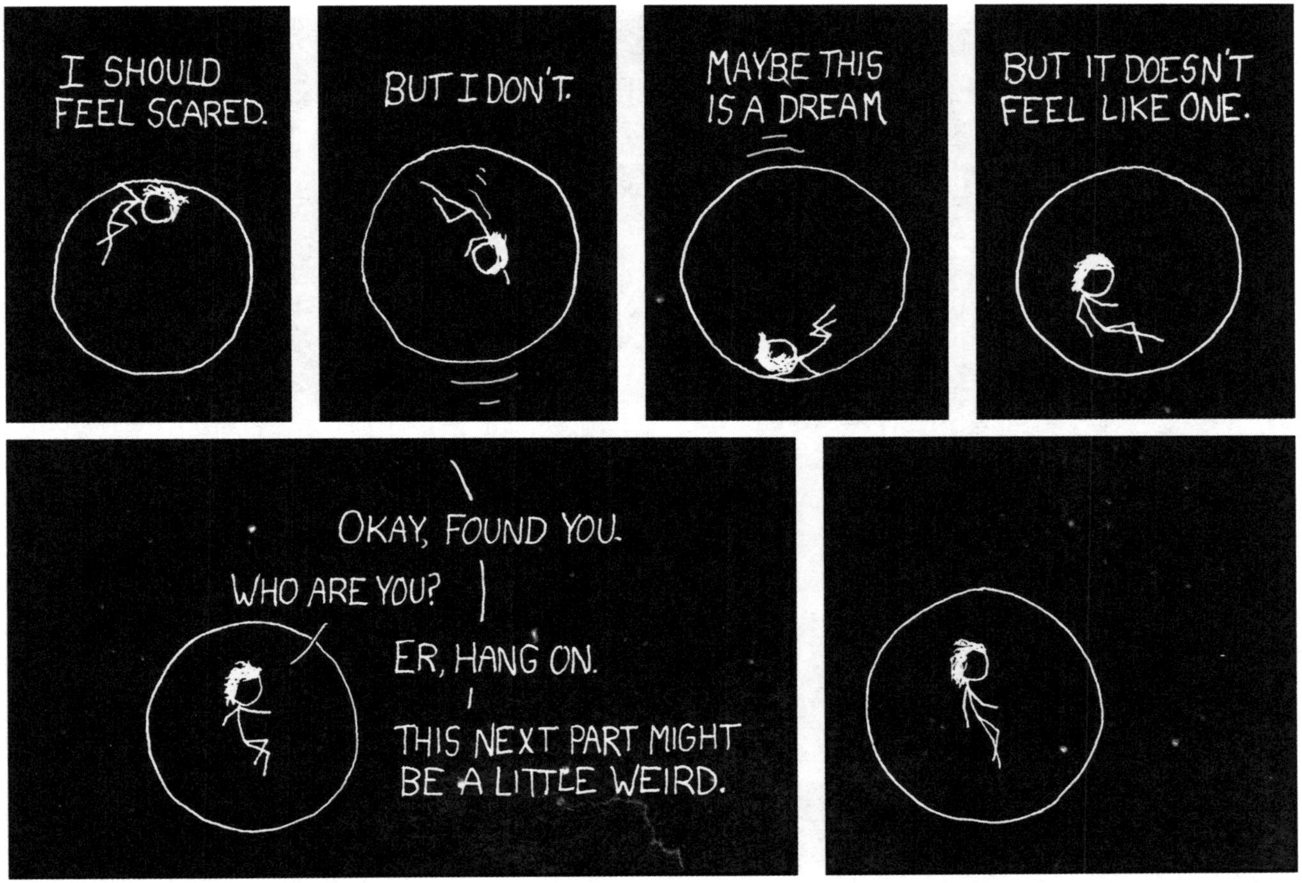
I SHOULD FEEL SCARED.
BUT I DON'T.
MAYBE THIS IS A DREAM
BUT IT DOESN'T FEEL LIKE ONE.
OKAY, FOUND YOU.
WHO ARE YOU?
ER, HANG ON.
THIS NEXT PART MIGHT BE A LITTLE WEIRD.

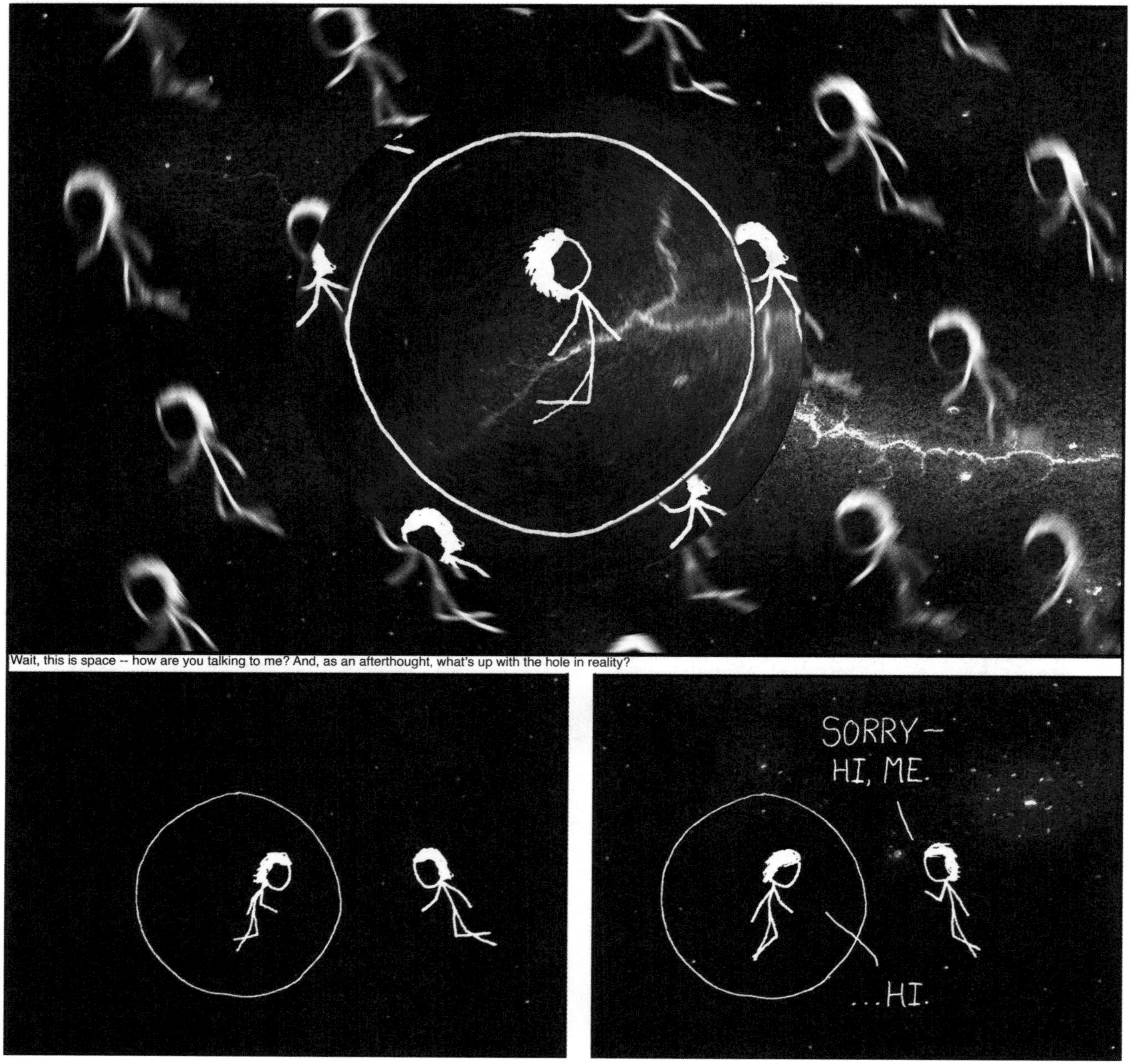
Wait, this is space -- how are you talking to me? And, as an afterthought, what's up with the hole in reality?
SORRY—
HI, ME.
...HI.

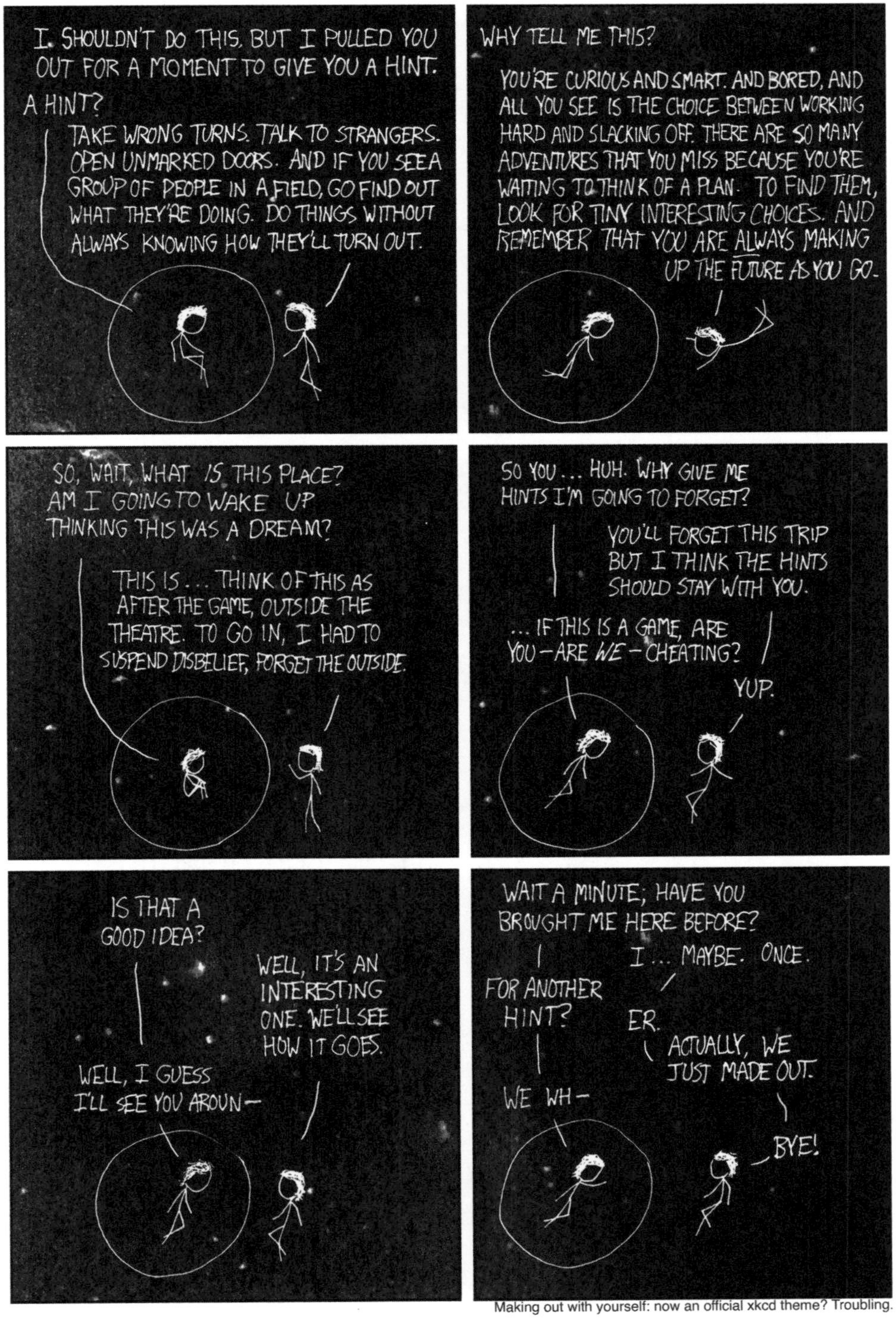
I SHOULDN'T DO THIS, BUT I PULLED YOU OUT FOR A MOMENT TO GIVE YOU A HINT.
A HINT?
TAKE WRONG TURNS. TALK TO STRANGERS. OPEN UNMARKED DOORS. AND IF YOU SEE A GROUP OF PEOPLE IN A FIELD, GO FIND OUT WHAT THEY'RE DOING. DO THINGS WITHOUT ALWAYS KNOWING HOW THEY'LL TURN OUT.
WHY TELL ME THIS?
YOU'RE CURIOUS AND SMART. AND BORED, AND ALL YOU SEE IS THE CHOICE BETWEEN WORKING HARD AND SLACKING OFF. THERE ARE SO MANY ADVENTURES THAT YOU MISS BECAUSE YOU'RE WAITING TO THINK OF A PLAN. TO FIND THEM, LOOK FOR TINY INTERESTING CHOICES. AND REMEMBER THAT YOU ARE ALWAYS MAKING UP THE FUTURE AS YOU GO.
SO, WAIT, WHAT IS THIS PLACE? AM I GOING TO WAKE UP THINKING THIS WAS A DREAM?
THIS IS... THINK OF THIS AS AFTER THE GAME, OUTSIDE THE THEATRE. TO GO IN, I HAD TO SUSPEND DISBELIEF, FORGET THE OUTSIDE.
SO YOU... HUH. WHY GIVE ME HINTS I'M GOING TO FORGET?
YOU'LL FORGET THIS TRIP BUT I THINK THE HINTS SHOULD STAY WITH YOU.
... IF THIS IS A GAME, ARE YOU — ARE WE — CHEATING?
YUP.
IS THAT A GOOD IDEA?
WELL, IT'S AN INTERESTING ONE. WE'LL SEE HOW IT GOES.
WELL, I GUESS I'LL SEE YOU AROUN—
WAIT A MINUTE; HAVE YOU BROUGHT ME HERE BEFORE?
I... MAYBE. ONCE.
FOR ANOTHER HINT?
ER.
ACTUALLY, WE JUST MADE OUT.
WE WH—
BYE!

Making out with yourself: now an official xkcd theme? Troubling.

HI.
UH, HI.
SORRY IF THIS IS WEIRD, BUT
DO YOU LIKE FLYING KITES?

I wonder what percentage of not-obviously-busy people on the street would say yes to kite-flying with a stranger. This looks like a job for Science!

HALF OF WHAT YOU SEEK IS HERE / AND HALF YOU'VE SEEN BEFORE

WOW – ENGINES CAN BURN VEGETABLE OIL.
WELL, SURE. YOU CAN BURN MOST ANY ORGANIC MATTER. CORNS, LEAVES, SPICES...
SPICES? REALLY?
SURE – MUSSOLINI MADE THE TRAINS RUN ON THYME.
...
WE ARE NO LONGER FRIENDS.
I have nothing to apologize for.

429C6822BE41C334BE616EFF8B5A320

SO WHY DON'T YOU WISE UP A BIT / AND DIGG A LITTLE MORE

100000

ADVANTAGES TO DATING LIBRARIANS
WE'RE STOPPING IN BALTIMORE TO VISIT MY FAMILY, AND THAT'S FINAL.
OH YEAH?
HEY, LOOK, IT'S A NEW HARDBACK BOOK!
YOU WOULDN'T.
CRINKLE
CREAK
TWITCH
CRACK
OKAY!
YOU WIN!
Don't expect any leniency on late fees, though.

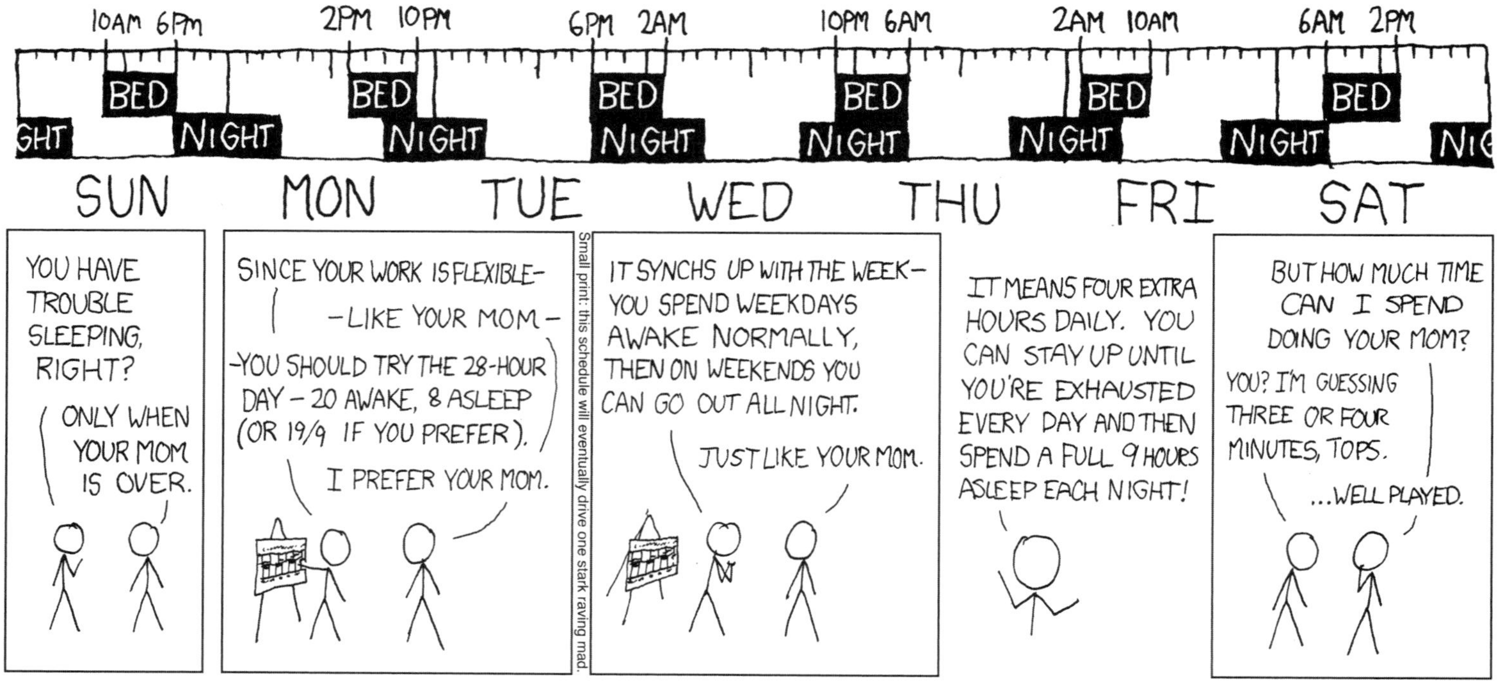
10AM 6PM
2PM 10PM
6PM 2AM
10PM 6AM
2AM 10AM
6AM 2PM
BED
NIGHT
SUN
MON
TUE
WED
THU
FRI
SAT
YOU HAVE TROUBLE SLEEPING, RIGHT?
ONLY WHEN YOUR MOM IS OVER.
SINCE YOUR WORK IS FLEXIBLE-
-LIKE YOUR MOM-
-YOU SHOULD TRY THE 28-HOUR DAY - 20 AWAKE, 8 ASLEEP (OR 19/9 IF YOU PREFER).
I PREFER YOUR MOM.
IT SYNCHS UP WITH THE WEEK- YOU SPEND WEEKDAYS AWAKE NORMALLY, THEN ON WEEKENDS YOU CAN GO OUT ALL NIGHT.
JUST LIKE YOUR MOM.
IT MEANS FOUR EXTRA HOURS DAILY. YOU CAN STAY UP UNTIL YOU'RE EXHAUSTED EVERY DAY AND THEN SPEND A FULL 9 HOURS ASLEEP EACH NIGHT!
BUT HOW MUCH TIME CAN I SPEND DOING YOUR MOM?
YOU? I'M GUESSING THREE OR FOUR MINUTES, TOPS.
...WELL PLAYED.
Small print: this schedule will eventually drive one stark raving mad.

100001

MY NEIGHBOR HAS LOUD SEX.
OHHHHHH
GASP
AAAAAAA
GOOD FOR HER AND ALL, BUT IT KEEPS ME UP AT NIGHT.
AND SHE'S SO SMUG ABOUT IT.
SORRY, COULD YOU HEAR US LAST NIGHT? OH, YOU KNOW HOW IT GETS SOMETIMES.
NOT REALLY...
BUT TONIGHT I FINALLY GET MY REVENGE.
BECAUSE NOW I HAVE A LOUD GIRLFRIEND TOO.
LOUD
AND AN ELLIPTICAL REFLECTOR DISH.
OOHHHHHHHHHHHHHHHHHHHHHHHHHHHHHHHHHHHHHHH
OHHH
YES YES YES YES YES YES YES YES YES YES YES YES YES
OH GOD OH GOD OH GOD OH GOD OH GOD OH GOD OH GOD OHGODOH
AAAAAAAAAAAHHHHHHHHHHHHHHHHHHHHHHHHHHHHH

Spherical or parabolic reflectors would of course lead to aberrant behavior.

HEY, A TAPE MEASURE.
EXTEND
EXTEND
CLATTER
CLICK
SCHWOOP
EXTEND
EXTEND
EXTEND
OOH, EIGHT FEET. I WONDER IF THAT'S A RECORD.
GOOO!
GOOOO!
GOOOOOOOOO!!
EXTEND
EXTEND
EXTEND

This sequence was later reproduced in the International Tape-Extending Federation archives, retitled 'The Founding of the Sport'.

MY HOBBY:
EMBEDDING NP-COMPLETE PROBLEMS IN RESTAURANT ORDERS
CHOTCHKIES RESTAURANT
APPETIZERS
MIXED FRUIT 2.15
FRENCH FRIES 2.75
SIDE SALAD 3.35
HOT WINGS 3.55
MOZZARELLA STICKS 4.20
SAMPLER PLATE 5.80
SANDWICHES
WE'D LIKE EXACTLY $15.05 WORTH OF APPETIZERS, PLEASE.
... EXACTLY? UHH ...
HERE, THESE PAPERS ON THE KNAPSACK PROBLEM MIGHT HELP YOU OUT.
LISTEN, I HAVE SIX OTHER TABLES TO GET TO –
– AS FAST AS POSSIBLE, OF COURSE. WANT SOMETHING ON TRAVELING SALESMAN?
General solutions get you a 50% tip.

I WROTE A PERL SCRIPT TO GENERATE SETS OF PRICES WITH ONLY ONE SOLUTION. BUT THE SCRIPT HAD A BUG (YOU CAN'T COMPARE IEEE FLOATS FOR EQUALITY) SO THERE ARE ACTUALLY TWO, AND ONE IS EASY (7 MIXED FRUITS).

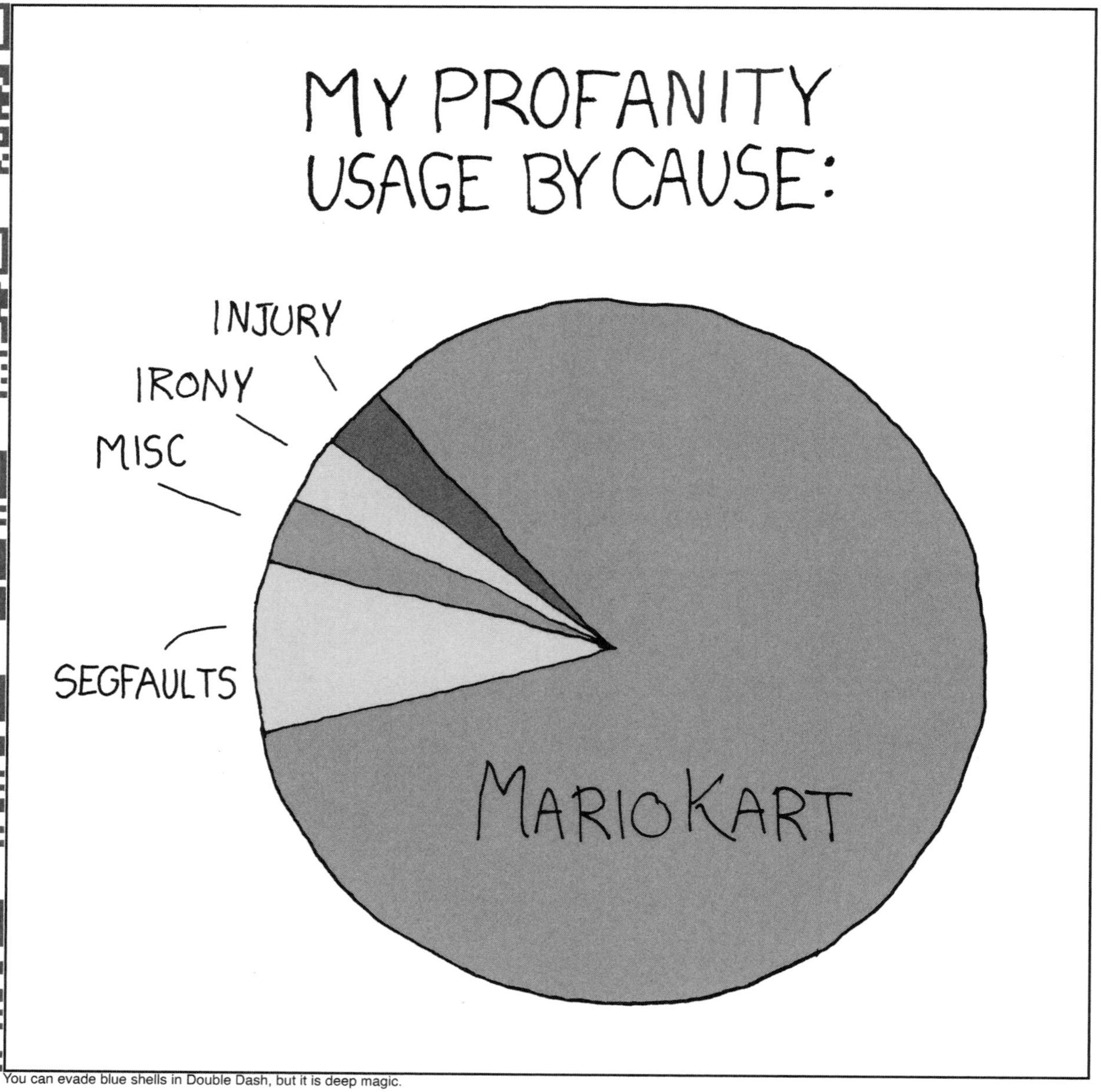
MY PROFANITY
USAGE BY CAUSE:
INJURY
IRONY
MISC
SEGFAULTS
MARIOKART

You can evade blue shells in Double Dash, but it is deep magic.

THE #1 PROGRAMMER EXCUSE FOR LEGITIMATELY SLACKING OFF:
"MY CODE'S COMPILING."
HEY! GET BACK TO WORK!
COMPILING!
OH. CARRY ON.

'Are you stealing those LCDs?' 'Yeah, but I'm doing it while my code compiles.'

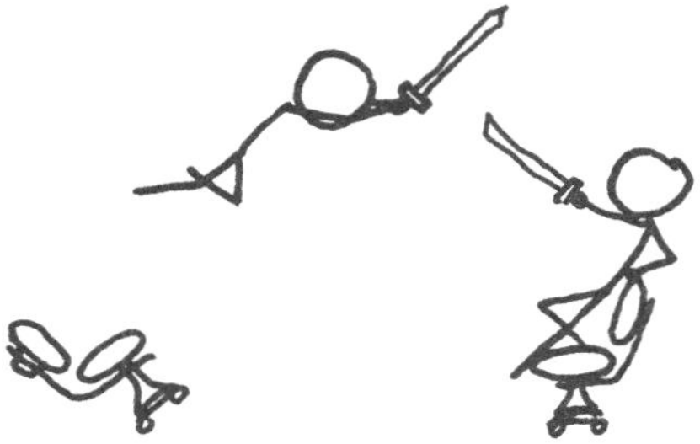

YOU WERE ONCE SHOVED HEADFIRST THROUGH SOMEONE'S VAGINA. WHY ARE YOU ACTING SO DIGNIFIED?

'I don't know, why is your beret staying on your head?' 'Staples.'

100020

HUH— THOMAS THE TANK ENGINE SLASH FICTION.
IT'S RULE 34 OF THE INTERNET: IF YOU CAN IMAGINE IT, THERE IS PORN OF IT.
NAH. THE WEB IS FREAKY, BUT IT CAN'T BEGIN TO HAVE EVERYTHING.
THERE'S NO PORN SET ATOP STORM-CHASING VANS. NO HOMOEROTIC SPELLING BEES. NO WOMEN PLAYING ELECTRIC GUITAR IN THE SHOWER.
ACTUALLY, THAT LAST ONE WOULD LOOK PRETTY HOT. AS LONG AS THEY WERE UNPLUGGED OR WATERPROOFED...
RIVULETS OF WATER RUN DOWN HER CHEST, THE SMOOTH BODY OF THE GUITAR FIRM AGAINST HER HIPS.
SHE TWANGS THE E-STRING AND IT SHAKES OFF TINY DROPLETS IN ALL DIRECTIONS.
YOU'RE SURE IT DOESN'T EXIST?
NOT YET.
I'M REGISTERING WETRIFFS.COM. LET'S GET ON THIS.
Okay, Lance. For entry into the college bowl, spell 'Throbbing'.

HI, THIS IS YOUR SON'S SCHOOL. WE'RE HAVING SOME COMPUTER TROUBLE.
OH, DEAR – DID HE BREAK SOMETHING?
IN A WAY–
DID YOU REALLY NAME YOUR SON Robert'); DROP TABLE Students;-- ?
OH. YES. LITTLE BOBBY TABLES, WE CALL HIM.
WELL, WE'VE LOST THIS YEAR'S STUDENT RECORDS. I HOPE YOU'RE HAPPY.
AND I HOPE YOU'VE LEARNED TO SANITIZE YOUR DATABASE INPUTS.
Her daughter is named Help I'm trapped in a driver's license factory.

Foreplay
From Wikipedia
Wikipedia
Wikipedia's role as brain-extension, while a little troubling, is also really cool.

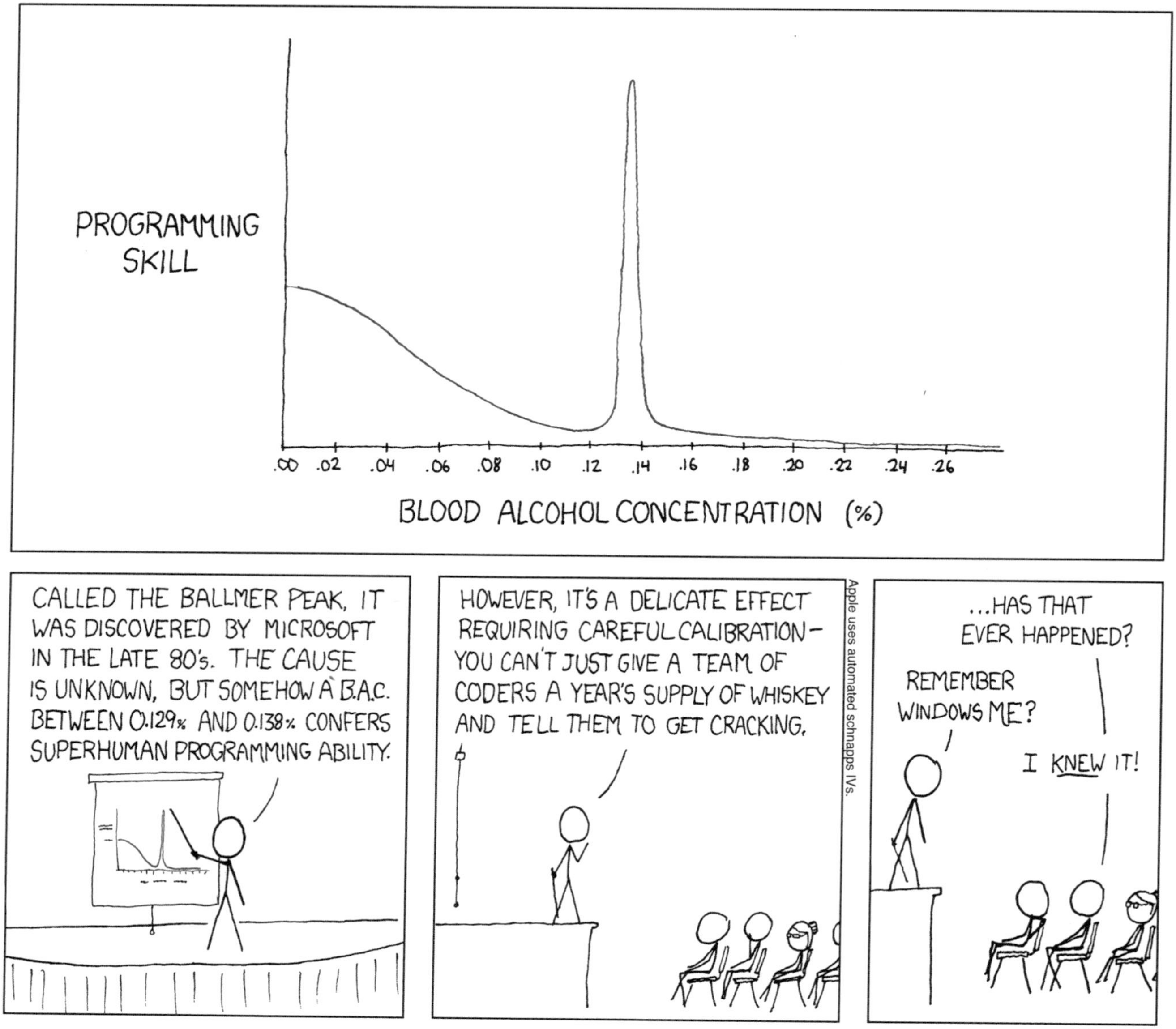
PROGRAMMING SKILL
.00 .02 .04 .06 .08 .10 .12 .14 .16 .18 .20 .22 .24 .26
BLOOD ALCOHOL CONCENTRATION (%)
CALLED THE BALLMER PEAK, IT WAS DISCOVERED BY MICROSOFT IN THE LATE 80's. THE CAUSE IS UNKNOWN, BUT SOMEHOW A B.A.C. BETWEEN 0.129% AND 0.138% CONFERS SUPERHUMAN PROGRAMMING ABILITY.
HOWEVER, IT'S A DELICATE EFFECT REQUIRING CAREFUL CALIBRATION— YOU CAN'T JUST GIVE A TEAM OF CODERS A YEAR'S SUPPLY OF WHISKEY AND TELL THEM TO GET CRACKING.
Apple uses automated schnapps IVs.
...HAS THAT EVER HAPPENED?
REMEMBER WINDOWS ME?
I KNEW IT!

IF YOU LOOK CAREFULLY, THE PRECISE LOCATION OF THE PEAK SHOULD NOT COME AS A SURPRISE.

100102

HI. I'M HERE ABOUT THE GIRL WHO VISITED YOUR IRC CHANNEL LAST NIGHT LOOKING FOR JAVA HELP.
WHAT DID YOU DO TO MY DOOR?
WHEN SOMEONE WITH A FEMININE USERNAME JOINS YOUR COMMUNITY, AND YOU SAY "OMG A WOMAN ON THE INTERNET" AND 'JOKINGLY' ASK FOR NAKED PICS, YOU ARE BEING AN ASSHOLE. YOU ARE NOT BEING IRONIC. YOU ARE NOT CRACKING EVERYBODY UP. YOU ARE THE NUMBER ONE REASON WOMEN ARE SO RARE ON THE INTERNET.
AT LEAST, THE PARTS OF IT YOU FREQUENT.
AS SOMEONE WHO LIKES NERDY GIRLS, I DO NOT APPRECIATE THIS. I'M HERE TO BAN YOU FROM THE INTERNET. THE GAL BEHIND ME WITH THE EMP CANNON IS JOANNA – SHE'LL BE ASSIGNED TO YOU FOR THE NEXT YEAR. TRY TO GO ONLINE AND SHE'LL MELT YOUR PC.
DUDE, SHE'S HOT. IS SHE SINGLE?
JOANNA, FIRE.

But one of the regulars in the channel is a girl!

WHAT ARE YOU DOING?
MAKING THE WORLD A WEIRDER PLACE.
MRROWLLL
STARTING WITH MY EBAY FEEDBACK PAGE.
COMMENTS:
INSTEAD OF OFFICE CHAIR PACKAGE CONTAINED BOBCAT.
WOULD NOT BUY AGAIN.

You can do this once in every 30 times and still have 97% positive feedback.

WE HAD A FIGHT LAST NIGHT.
I GUESS SHE'S STILL MAD.
I WOKE UP TO FIND SHE'D WRITTEN A SAPPY LOVE NOTE
TO MY BOOT SECTOR.
OPERATING SYSTEM NOT FOUND
And she put sweet nothings in all my .conf files. It'll take me forever to get X working again.

THERE'S A CERTAIN TYPE OF BRAIN THAT'S EASILY DISABLED.
IF YOU SHOW IT AN INTERESTING PROBLEM, IT INVOLUNTARILY DROPS EVERYTHING ELSE TO WORK ON IT.
THIS HAS LED ME TO INVENT A NEW SPORT: NERD SNIPING.
SEE THAT PHYSICIST CROSSING THE ROAD?
HEY!
On this infinite grid of ideal one-ohm resistors,
what's the equivalent resistance between the two marked nodes?
I first saw this problem on a Google Labs Aptitude Test. A professor and I filled a blackboard without getting anywhere. Have fun.

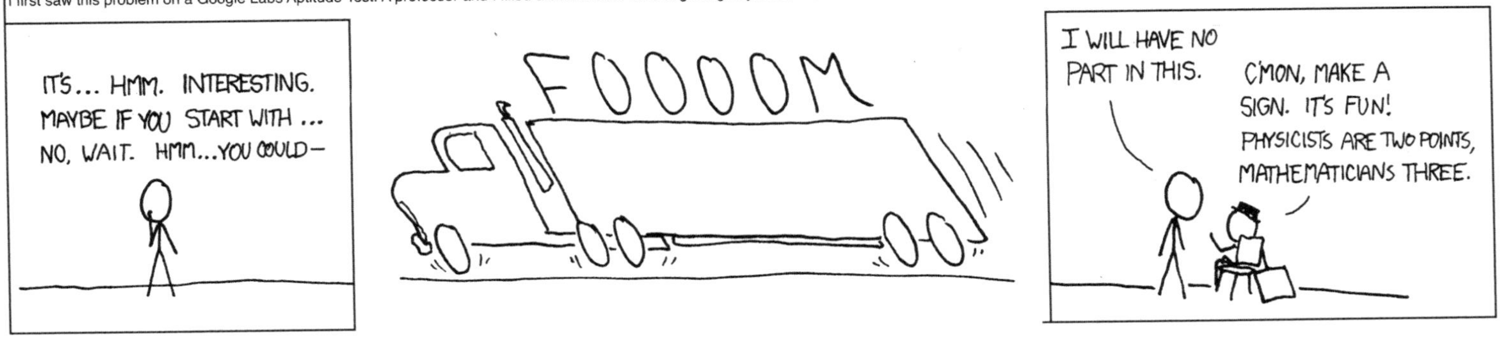
IT'S... HMM. INTERESTING. MAYBE IF YOU START WITH ... NO, WAIT. HMM...YOU COULD–
FOOOOM
I WILL HAVE NO PART IN THIS.
C'MON, MAKE A SIGN. IT'S FUN! PHYSICISTS ARE TWO POINTS, MATHEMATICIANS THREE.

100112

AS A PROJECT WEARS ON, STANDARDS FOR SUCCESS SLIP LOWER AND LOWER.
0 HOURS
OKAY, I SHOULD BE ABLE TO DUAL-BOOT BSD SOON.
6 HOURS
I'LL BE HAPPY IF I CAN GET THE SYSTEM WORKING LIKE IT WAS WHEN I STARTED.
10 HOURS
WELL, THE DESKTOP'S A LOST CAUSE, BUT I THINK I CAN FIX THE PROBLEMS THE LAPTOP'S DEVELOPED.
24 HOURS
IF WE'RE LUCKY, THE SHARKS WILL STAY AWAY UNTIL WE REACH SHALLOW WATER.
IF WE MAKE IT BACK ALIVE, YOU'RE NEVER UPGRADING ANYTHING AGAIN.

40% of OpenBSD installs lead to shark attacks. It's their only standing security issue.

BZZZZZZZ

100120

YEAH? WELL, YOUR MOM TURNS EVERY CONVERSATION INTO A "YOUR MOM" JOKE AND IT'S BECOME UNBEARABLE.
I'M SERIOUS; I CAN'T TAKE THIS ANYMORE. I'M LEAVING.
... THAT'S WHAT SHE SAID!
YES. YES, IT IS.

Yes, I mean she said that during sex. Yes, it was a little weird.

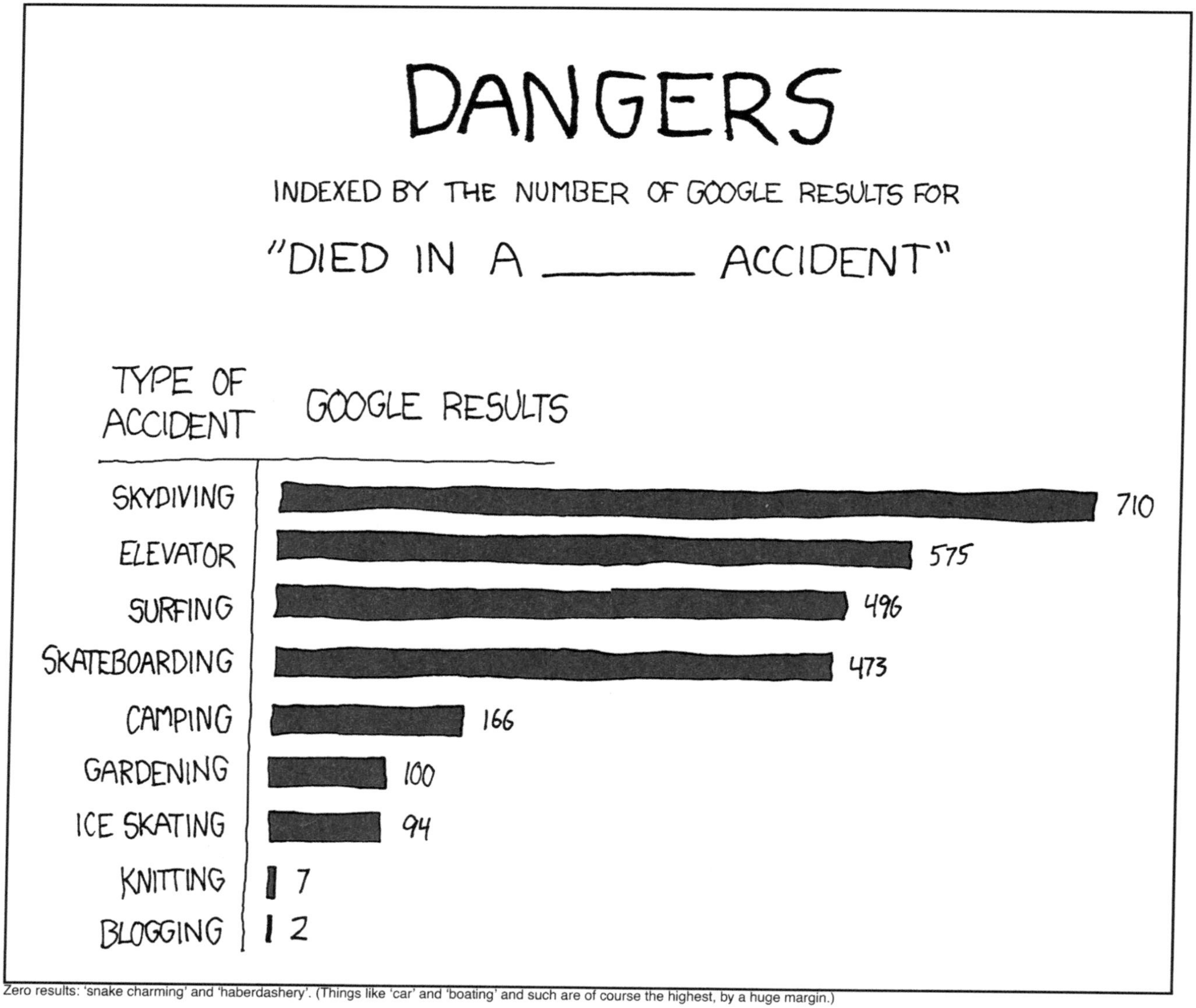
DANGERS
INDEXED BY THE NUMBER OF GOOGLE RESULTS FOR
"DIED IN A _____ ACCIDENT"
TYPE OF ACCIDENT
GOOGLE RESULTS
SKYDIVING
710
ELEVATOR
575
SURFING
496
SKATEBOARDING
473
CAMPING
166
GARDENING
100
ICE SKATING
94
KNITTING
7
BLOGGING
2

Zero results: 'snake charming' and 'haberdashery'. (Things like 'car' and 'boating' and such are of course the highest, by a huge margin.)

Or so I hope.

SINCE WHEN DO YOU KEEP A JOURNAL?
OH, I PRETEND TO WRITE IN IT ON THE TRAIN, AND WAIT FOR A SHY-LOOKING GIRL TO SIT ACROSS FROM ME.
And the journal is filled with all the things I'd say to her if I were nice like you. I burn it when it's full.
I GLANCE UP AND WAIT FOR HER TO MAKE EYE CONTACT, THEN LOOK DOWN BASHFULLY AND, IF I CAN, BLUSH.
THEN, WHEN I SEE HER START TO SMILE AT ME, I ROLL MY EYES AND HIT HER WITH A QUICK GLARE, THEN RESUME WRITING.
THE ALIENATION STAYS WITH HER ALL DAY. IT'S GREAT.
YOU'RE SICKENING. THIS IS WHY WE CAN'T HAVE NICE PEOPLE.
I CAN'T HELP IT. IT'S LIKE SHOOTING LONELY, ANGSTY FISH IN A BARREL.

BLUSH
I SEE WHAT YOU DID THERE.
YOU WERE TRYING TO OPEN ME UP SO YOU COULD HURT MY FEELINGS.
YOU LIKE TO HURT PEOPLE.
WELL, I LIKE TO HURT PEOPLE, TOO.
AND YOU KNOW WHAT?
I'm better at it than you.
I'M ABOUT TO HURT YOU MORE THAN YOU COULD EVER HURT ME.
SEE, I JUST SAW RIGHT THROUGH YOU.
ALONE OF ALL THE PEOPLE YOU'LL EVER MEET, I UNDERSTAND YOU—
—AND YOU'LL NEVER SEE ME AGAIN.
That's my hat! You took my hat!

101002

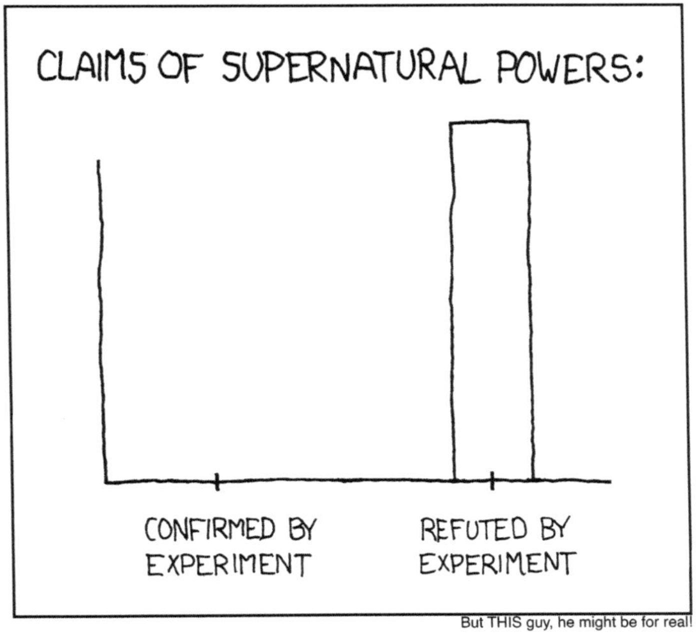
CLAIMS OF SUPERNATURAL POWERS:
CONFIRMED BY EXPERIMENT
REFUTED BY EXPERIMENT

But THIS guy, he might be for real!

WEIRD — MY CODE'S CRASHING WHEN GIVEN PRE-1970 DATES.
EPOCH FAIL!

The universe started in 1970. Anyone claiming to be over 38 is lying about their age.

-!- OPENING CHAT WITH BSLSK05
<NICKM> HI!
<NICKM> A/S/L?
TYPE TYPE
<BSLSK05> :)
05 > :)

U+FDD0 is actually Unicode for the eye of the basilisk, though for safety reasons no font actually renders it.

IT'S NEAT HOW YOU CONTAIN A FACTORY FOR MAKING MORE OF YOU.

We are sexy, sexy Von Neumann machines.

ARE YOU COMING TO BED?
I CAN'T. THIS IS IMPORTANT.
WHAT?
SOMEONE IS WRONG ON THE INTERNET.

What do you want me to do? LEAVE? Then they'll keep being wrong!

BOO!
FWUMP

SCOOCH
SCOOCH
SCOOCH

MY HOBBY:
PAUSING IN-STORE MUSIC FOR A SPLIT SECOND AND WATCHING THE EX-MARCHING BAND KIDS STUMBLE.
CLICK CLICK
FWOMP

You can identify them ahead-of-time -- they lead with their left foot when the music starts.

THANKS TO JAMES ZETLEN, WHO ARRANGED THE LOVELY PIECE IN THE COMIC FOR ME.

101012

CAN A NINJA CATCH AN ARROW? ON THIS EPISODE, WE'LL FIND OUT!
MMM, SCIENCE.
HEY, MYTHBUSTERS IS ENTERTAINING, BUT IT'S NOT SCIENCE.
BRAAAAAI''INNS...
ZOMBIE FEYNMAN!
YOU GOT A PROBLEM WITH MYTHBUSTERS?
THEY FAIL AT BASIC RIGOR!
"IDEAS ARE TESTED BY EXPERIMENT." THAT IS THE CORE OF SCIENCE. EVERYTHING ELSE IS BOOKKEEPING.
BY TEACHING PEOPLE TO HOLD THEIR BELIEFS UP TO EXPERIMENT, MYTHBUSTERS IS DOING MORE TO DRAG HUMANITY OUT OF THE UNSCIENTIFIC DARKNESS THAN A THOUSAND LESSONS IN RIGOR.
SHOW THEM SOME LOVE.
ANYWAY, BACK TO ZOMBIE STUFF. I HUNGER FOR BRAAAAAAIIINNS!
UH, TRY THE PHYSICS LAB NEXT DOOR.
I SAID BRAINS. ALL THEY'VE GOT ARE STRING THEORISTS.

Last week, we busted the myth that electroweak gauge symmetry is broken by the higgs mechanism. We'll also examine the existence of God and whether true love exists.

YOU JUST WON THE GAME.
IT'S OKAY! YOU'RE FREE!

I'm as surprised as you! I didn't think it was possible.

DEATH?
SPEAKING.
THIS IS THE BOSS. WHERE ARE YOU? YOU HAVEN'T BEEN TO THE OFFICE IN DAYS!
I'VE BEEN HELD UP.
WHAT HAPPENED?
YOU KNOW HOW WHEN SOMEONE DIES, THEY CAN CHALLENGE ME TO A GAME FOR THEIR SOUL?
SURE, STANDARD PROCEDURE.
WELL, WE DIDN'T COUNT ON THIS GUY. I MIGHT BE A WHILE.
I ADD THE PALADIN TO MY PARTY.
OH, JESUS, HE'S GETTING OUT ANOTHER RULEBOOK.

RIP, Gary.

STARTING WIFI AUTOCONFIG... SEARCHING FOR WIFI... FOUND NO OPEN NETWORKS.
FOUND SECURE NET SSID "Lenhart Family"
TRYING COMMON PASSWORDS... FAILED.
CHECKING FOR WEP VULNERABILITIES...
UM.
NONE FOUND.
CONNECTING TO BLUETOOTH PHONE...
CALLING LOCAL SCHOOL...
FOUND LENHART CHILDREN.
NOTIFYING FIELD AGENTS. CHILDREN ACQUIRED. CALLING LENHART PARENTS. NEGOTIATING FOR WIFI PASSWORD...
CTRL-C
CTRL-C

I hear this is an option in the latest Ubuntu release.

YOU WATCHED THE TAPE!?
YEAH, SORRY.
NOW YOU'LL DIE IN SEVEN DAYS!
IT'S WORSE THAN THAT.
... YOU DIDN'T.
YUP.
On the other hand, poor Samara -- transcoded to FLV. No one deserves that.
GREAT, IT'S GOT 363,104 VIEWS ALREADY.
THEY KEPT RICKROLLING ME!
IT WAS ONLY FAIR.

I'D TAP THAT ASS
TO BE THE NEW COMMITTEE CHAIR.
I'D TAP THAT ASS
WITHOUT A WARRANT.
I'D TAP THAT ASS
AND EXTRACT DELICIOUS MAPLE SYRUP.
Hey, when you're done draining the syrup, just leave the hole, okay?
I'D HAVE SEX WITH THAT TREE.

MMM, I'M GETTING WOOD.
CENSORED
YEARS PASS
SON OF A BEECH!

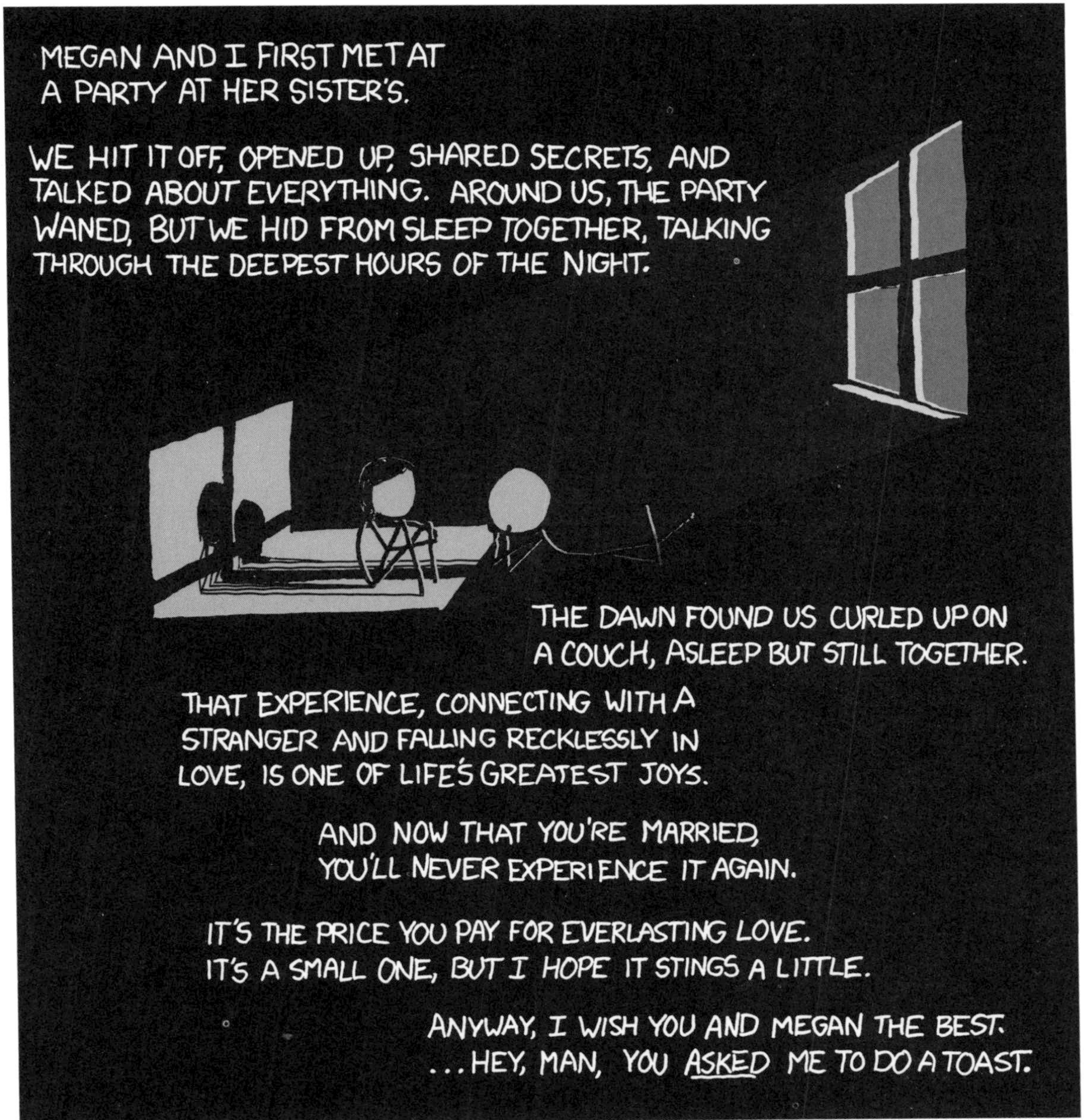
MEGAN AND I FIRST MET AT A PARTY AT HER SISTER'S.
WE HIT IT OFF, OPENED UP, SHARED SECRETS, AND TALKED ABOUT EVERYTHING. AROUND US, THE PARTY WANED, BUT WE HID FROM SLEEP TOGETHER, TALKING THROUGH THE DEEPEST HOURS OF THE NIGHT.
THE DAWN FOUND US CURLED UP ON A COUCH, ASLEEP BUT STILL TOGETHER.
THAT EXPERIENCE, CONNECTING WITH A STRANGER AND FALLING RECKLESSLY IN LOVE, IS ONE OF LIFE'S GREATEST JOYS.
AND NOW THAT YOU'RE MARRIED, YOU'LL NEVER EXPERIENCE IT AGAIN.
IT'S THE PRICE YOU PAY FOR EVERLASTING LOVE. IT'S A SMALL ONE, BUT I HOPE IT STINGS A LITTLE.
ANYWAY, I WISH YOU AND MEGAN THE BEST. ...HEY, MAN, YOU ASKED ME TO DO A TOAST.
Oh, huh, so you didn't know that story?

101102

IF ONLY THERE WERE SOME WAY WE COULD BE TOGETHER.
WE'RE SO LUCKY TO HAVE EACH OTHER. HOW DID IT HAPPEN, ANYWAY?
I, UHH... I DON'T REMEMBER.
NO, REALLY, HOW DID WE GET TOGETHER? IT'S HARD TO IMAGINE IT HAPPENING.
IT DOES STRAIN THE BOUNDS OF FANTASY...
...FANTASY? THAT'S IT!
MY GOD, IT'S THE ONLY EXPLANATION: WE'RE OBJECTS IN SOME TRANSIENT FANTASY. WE'LL BE GONE WHEN IT ENDS!
WE'LL LOSE EACH OTHER.
OH GOD.
WELL, I'M NOT GOING OUT QUIETLY. I'M BURNING THIS FUCKING WORLD.
BURN THE WORLD!
FIRE! FIRE! CLEANSE THIS HELLISH PLACE-
??

I guess if she accepted irrational realities, she'd hardly be my fantasy.

IF IT'S UNIMPORTANT ENOUGH TO BASICALLY WORK ON THE HONOR SYSTEM, IT'S NOT GONNA CRASH THE PLANE.
OKAY, WHAT AIRLINE?
I'M FOLLOWING YOU.
... I'M FOLLOWING YOU.
AIRPORT
I ASSUMED WE WERE WALKING TO A BAKERY.
YOU ALWAYS ASSUME THAT!
LOCKPICKS? THESE ARE ... ILLEGAL, ACTUALLY. WHERE DID YOU GET THEM?
YOU NEED TO COME WITH-
OH MAN, IT ALL STARTED WITH THIS HACKER GIRL.
SURE, SURE. BUT MAN, LET ME TELL YOU ABOUT HER!
IF YOUR DEVICE HAS A "TRANSMIT" FUNCTION, PLEASE DISABLE IT.
OKAY — HANG ON, I'M HALFWAY THROUGH THE IWCONFIG MAN PAGE.
SIR, IS THIS CONTAINER UNDER THREE OUNCES?
NOT SURE. HOW MUCH BLOOD IS THERE IN A CHURCHMOUSE?
... WHY DON'T YOU JUST GO.

Under three ounces, but it stains panties.

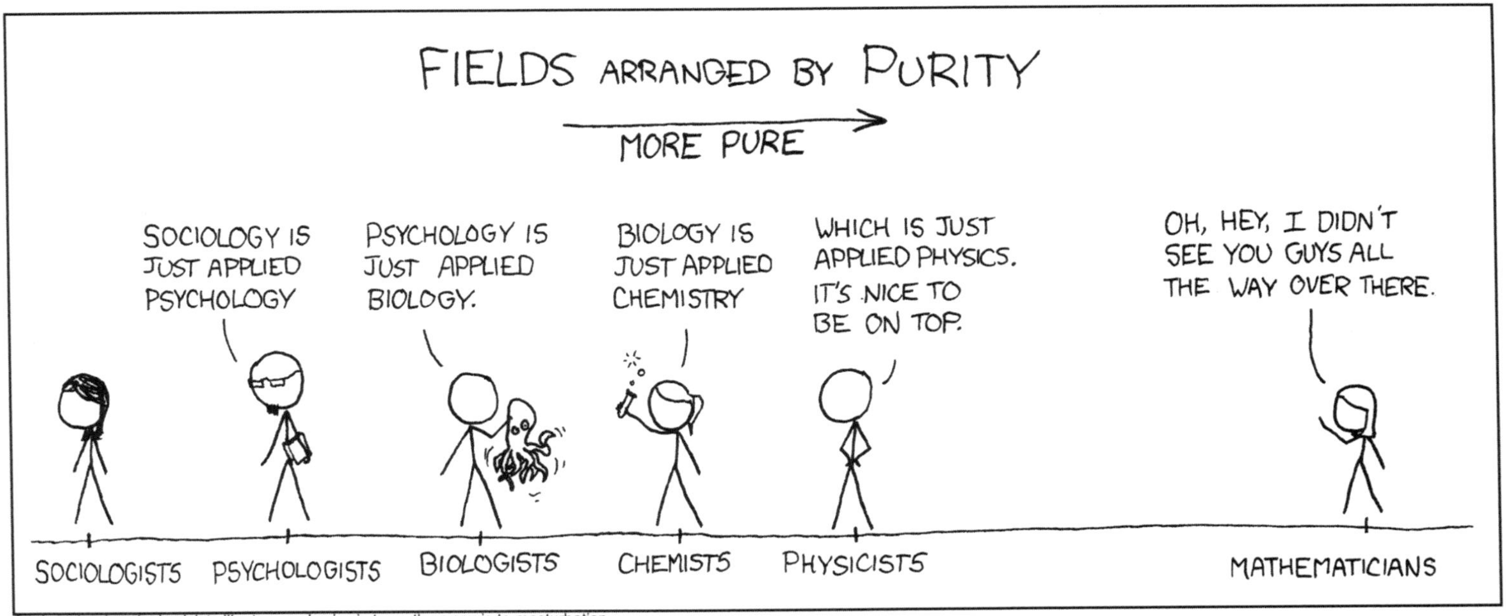
FIELDS ARRANGED BY PURITY
MORE PURE
SOCIOLOGY IS JUST APPLIED PSYCHOLOGY
PSYCHOLOGY IS JUST APPLIED BIOLOGY.
BIOLOGY IS JUST APPLIED CHEMISTRY
WHICH IS JUST APPLIED PHYSICS. IT'S NICE TO BE ON TOP.
OH, HEY, I DIDN'T SEE YOU GUYS ALL THE WAY OVER THERE.
SOCIOLOGISTS
PSYCHOLOGISTS
BIOLOGISTS
CHEMISTS
PHYSICISTS
MATHEMATICIANS

On the other hand, physicists like to say physics is to math as sex is to masturbation.

Bonus strip: just read the rightmost panels straight down.
I'M LEAVING YOU.

AS THE FORUMITES GLEEFULLY DISCOVERED, YOU CAN MAKE ALL SORTS OF STORIES JUST BY REARRANGING THESE PANELS.

101112

OH GOD
THE OZONE LAYER!
THAT WAS OUR LAST BANANA.
YOU'RE SUCH AN ASSHOLE.

An eternity later, the universe having turned out to have positive curvature and lots of mass, the boomerang hits him in the back of the head.

GU

MY HOBBY:
SITTING DOWN WITH GRAD STUDENTS AND TIMING HOW LONG IT TAKES THEM TO FIGURE OUT THAT I'M NOT ACTUALLY AN EXPERT IN THEIR FIELD.
ENGINEERING:
OUR BIG PROBLEM IS HEAT DISSIPATION
HAVE YOU TRIED LOGARITHMS?
48 SECONDS
LINGUISTICS:
AH, SO DOES THIS FINNO-UGRIC FAMILY INCLUDE, SAY, KLINGON?
63 SECONDS
SOCIOLOGY:
YEAH, MY LATEST WORK IS ON RANKING PEOPLE FROM BEST TO WORST.
4 MINUTES
LITERARY CRITICISM:
YOU SEE, THE DECONSTRUCTION IS INEXTRICABLE FROM NOT ONLY THE TEXT, BUT ALSO THE SELF.
EIGHT PAPERS AND TWO BOOKS AND THEY HAVEN'T CAUGHT ON.

If you think I'm being too hard on literary criticism, read the Wikipedia article on deconstruction.

OKAY, WE'RE IN THE BELLY OF THE MACHINE. YOU GOT THE CHARGES?
THE WHAT?
THE EXPLOSIVE CHARGES!
I JUST BROUGHT THIS BAG FOR PASTRIES.
THE HELL? WE'RE ON A MISSION HERE!
THIS ISN'T A BAKERY?
OH, CHRIST, NOT THIS SHIT AGAIN.
WHAT ABOUT THESE SCONES?
THOSE ARE LUG NUTS.
... MAYBE *SOME* OF THEM AREN'T!
CRUNCH
OW!
CRUNCH

Don't you know? The chances of a random object being a scone are about one in six.

PREMIER ELECTION SOLUTIONS (FORMERLY DIEBOLD) HAS BLAMED OHIO VOTING MACHINE ERRORS ON PROBLEMS WITH THE MACHINES' MCAFEE ANTIVIRUS SOFTWARE.
WAIT.
"ANTIVIRUS SOFTWARE"? ON VOTING MACHINES? *YOU'RE DOING IT WRONG.*
WHY? SECURITY IS GOOD, RIGHT?
OF COURSE. BUT, WELL–
IMAGINE YOU'RE AT A PARENT-TEACHER CONFERENCE, AND THE TEACHER REASSURES YOU THAT HE ALWAYS WEARS A CONDOM WHILE TEACHING.
AH. STRICTLY SPEAKING, IT'S BETTER THAN THE ALTERNATIVE–
–YET SOMEONE IS CLEARLY DOING THEIR JOB HORRIBLY WRONG.
And that's "another" crypto conference I've been kicked out of. C'mon, it's a great analogy!

IT'S OVER.
AFTER TWENTY MONTHS IT'S FINALLY OVER.
I DON'T HAVE TO BE AN ELECTION JUNKIE ANYMORE.
I DON'T HAVE TO CARE ABOUT OPINION POLLS, EXIT POLLS, MARGINS OF ERROR, ATTACK ADS, GAME-CHANGERS, TRACKING POLLS, SWING STATES, SWING VOTES, THE BRADLEY EFFECT, OR <NAME> THE <OCCUPATION>.
I'M FREE.
Google
2012 polling statistics
TAP TAP
Someday I'll be rich enough to hire Nate Silver to help make all my life decisions.
'Should I sleep with her?' 'Well, I'm showing a 35% chance it will end badly.'

WHAT ARE YOU WRITING?
VIRUS.
WHAT'S IT DO?
WHEN SOMEONE TRIES TO POST A YOUTUBE COMMENT, IT FIRST READS IT ALOUD BACK TO THEM.
SOON, EVERYWHERE:
TYPE TYPE TYPE
... I'M A MORON.
I...
I DIDN'T KNOW.
Man, I just wanted to know how babby was formed.

WE NEED TO TALK.
POW
SSSSS
COUGH
BEEP BEEP
BEEP BEEP BEEP BEEP
BEEP BEEP BEEP B
BEEP BEEP
RATTLE RATTLE
BEEP BEEP BEEP BEEP BEEP
BEEP BEEP BEEP BEEP BEE

The sad thing is that I just wanted to talk about your poor smoke-bomb techniques.

110002

XKCD PRESENTS
A GUIDE TO
NUMERICAL SEX POSITIONS
69
99
71
34
UH.
√8
GUYS?
We didn't even get to the continued fractions!
ln(2π)
AWW, C'MON...
HEY, BABY, WANNA TRY $\int_0^\infty t^{z-1}e^{-t}dt$ ING?

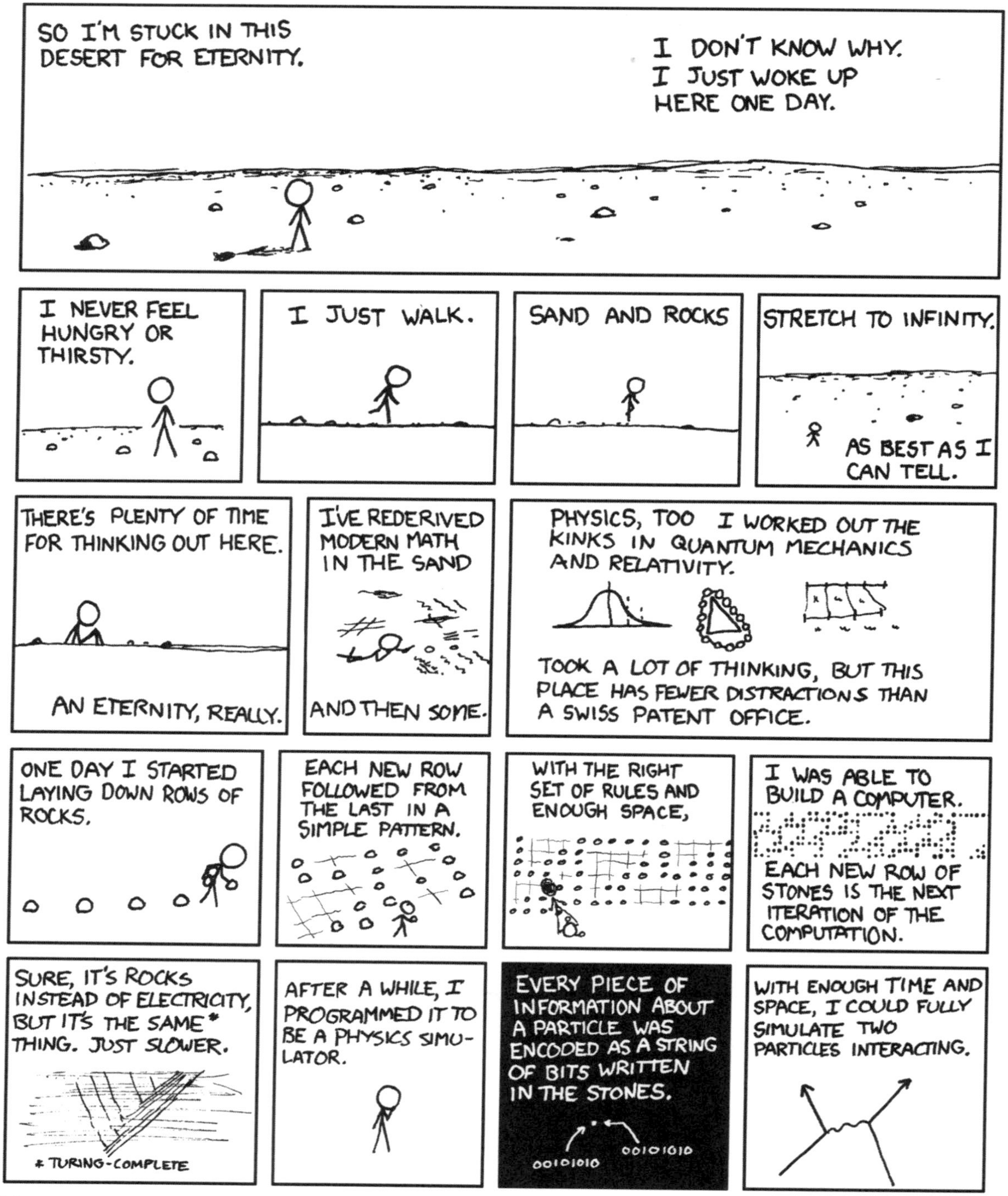
SO I'M STUCK IN THIS DESERT FOR ETERNITY.
I DON'T KNOW WHY. I JUST WOKE UP HERE ONE DAY.
I NEVER FEEL HUNGRY OR THIRSTY.
I JUST WALK.
SAND AND ROCKS
STRETCH TO INFINITY.
AS BEST AS I CAN TELL.
THERE'S PLENTY OF TIME FOR THINKING OUT HERE.
AN ETERNITY, REALLY.
I'VE REDERIVED MODERN MATH IN THE SAND
AND THEN SOME.
PHYSICS, TOO. I WORKED OUT THE KINKS IN QUANTUM MECHANICS AND RELATIVITY.
TOOK A LOT OF THINKING, BUT THIS PLACE HAS FEWER DISTRACTIONS THAN A SWISS PATENT OFFICE.
ONE DAY I STARTED LAYING DOWN ROWS OF ROCKS.
EACH NEW ROW FOLLOWED FROM THE LAST IN A SIMPLE PATTERN.
WITH THE RIGHT SET OF RULES AND ENOUGH SPACE,
I WAS ABLE TO BUILD A COMPUTER.
EACH NEW ROW OF STONES IS THE NEXT ITERATION OF THE COMPUTATION.
SURE, IT'S ROCKS INSTEAD OF ELECTRICITY, BUT IT'S THE SAME* THING. JUST SLOWER.
* TURING-COMPLETE
AFTER A WHILE, I PROGRAMMED IT TO BE A PHYSICS SIMU-LATOR.
EVERY PIECE OF INFORMATION ABOUT A PARTICLE WAS ENCODED AS A STRING OF BITS WRITTEN IN THE STONES.
00101010
00101010
WITH ENOUGH TIME AND SPACE, I COULD FULLY SIMULATE TWO PARTICLES INTERACTING.

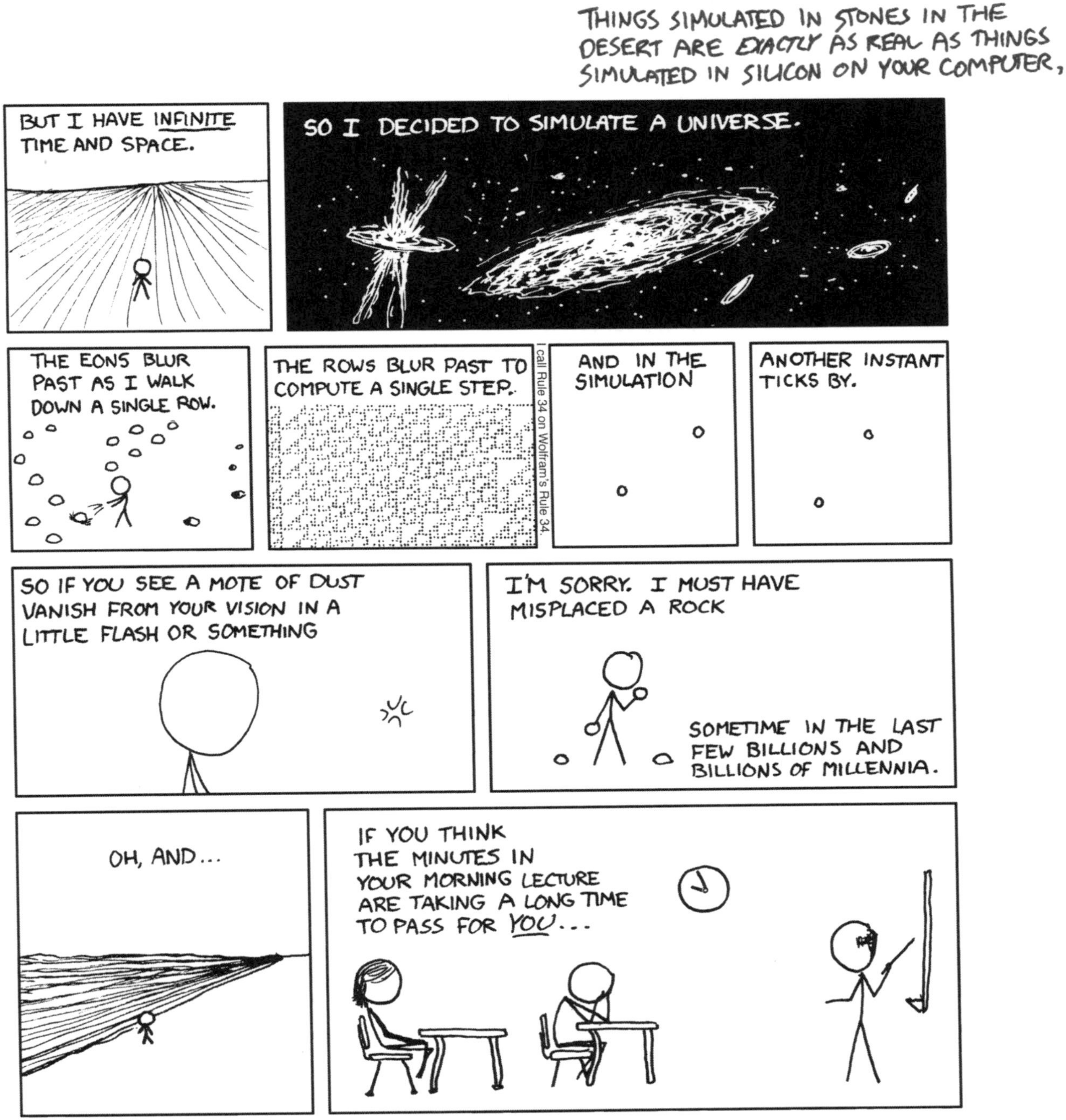

THINGS SIMULATED IN STONES IN THE DESERT ARE EXACTLY AS REAL AS THINGS SIMULATED IN SILICON ON YOUR COMPUTER,
BUT I HAVE INFINITE TIME AND SPACE.
SO I DECIDED TO SIMULATE A UNIVERSE.
THE EONS BLUR PAST AS I WALK DOWN A SINGLE ROW.
THE ROWS BLUR PAST TO COMPUTE A SINGLE STEP.
I call Rule 34 on Wolfram's Rule 34
AND IN THE SIMULATION
ANOTHER INSTANT TICKS BY.
SO IF YOU SEE A MOTE OF DUST VANISH FROM YOUR VISION IN A LITTLE FLASH OR SOMETHING
I'M SORRY. I MUST HAVE MISPLACED A ROCK
SOMETIME IN THE LAST FEW BILLIONS AND BILLIONS OF MILLENNIA.
OH, AND...
IF YOU THINK THE MINUTES IN YOUR MORNING LECTURE ARE TAKING A LONG TIME TO PASS FOR YOU...

THINKING OF BUYING FROM AUDIBLE.COM OR iTUNES?
REMEMBER, IF YOU PIRATE SOMETHING, IT'S YOURS FOR LIFE. YOU CAN TAKE IT ANYWHERE AND IT WILL ALWAYS WORK.
BUY OR PIRATE
BUY
THINGS CHANGE
PIRATE
YOU'RE A CRIMINAL
YOU TRY TO RECOVER YOUR COLLECTION
BUT IF YOU BUY DRM-LOCKED MEDIA, AND YOU EVER SWITCH OPERATING SYSTEMS OR NEW TECHNOLOGY COMES ALONG, YOUR COLLECTION COULD BE LOST.
AND IF YOU TRY TO KEEP IT, YOU'LL BE A CRIMINAL (DMCA 1201).
SO REMEMBER: IF YOU WANT A COLLECTION YOU CAN COUNT ON, PIRATE IT.
HEY, YOU'LL BE A CRIMINAL EITHER WAY.
(IF YOU DON'T LIKE THIS, DEMAND DRM-FREE FILES)
HEY, TURNS OUT WE WON THIS ONE! GOOD JOB, ALL! PARTY AT MY PLACE?

I spent more time trying to get an audible.com audio book playing than it took to listen to the book. I have lost every other piece of DRM-locked music I have paid for.

THE WEATHER OUTSIDE IS FRIGHTFUL.
I HATE TRUDGING THROUGH THE ICY SLUSH AND BITING SLEET.
BUT IT BEATS LYING IN OUR WARM, COZY BED
LISTENING TO YOU TALK ABOUT DRM FOR HOURS ON END.
COME BACK! JUST LISTEN TO THIS ONE QUOTE FROM *FREE CULTURE*!

I mean, I can barely hear myself complaining about Battlestar Galactica.

SHOULD I ASK?
I'M LOCKED OUT, AND TRYING TO GET MY ROOMMATE TO LET ME IN.
FIRST I TRIED HER CELL PHONE, BUT IT'S OFF.
THEN I TRIED IRC, BUT SHE'S NOT ONLINE.
I COULDN'T FIND ANYTHING TO THROW AT HER WINDOW,
SO I SSH'D INTO THE MAC MINI IN THE LIVING ROOM AND GOT THE SPEECH SYNTH TO YELL TO HER FOR ME.
HEY I'M LOCKED OUT DOWNSTAIRS
BUT I THINK I LEFT THE VOLUME WAY DOWN, SO I'M READING THE OS X DOCS TO LEARN TO SET THE VOLUME VIA COMMAND LINE.
AH.
I TAKE IT THE DOORBELL DOESN'T WORK?

Sadly, this is a true story. At least I learned about the OS X 'say' command.

DO

I HAVE A CRUSH ON YOU.
I COULD ASK YOU OUT, AND MOVE ON WITH MY LIFE IF YOU SAID NO.
OR,
WE COULD BE FRIENDS!
SEE, I DON'T WANT TO CONSIDER THAT YOU MIGHT NOT BE ATTRACTED TO ME. I'M SCARED OF REJECTION, SO I'VE DECIDED RELATIONSHIPS SHOULD GROW SMOOTHLY OUT OF FRIENDSHIPS.
WHEN YOU HAVE PROBLEMS, I'LL BE THERE FOR YOU, NIGHT AFTER NIGHT.
SELFLESSLY.
HUG
I'LL TEAR DOWN THE JERKS YOU DATE, AND WAIT FOR YOU TO REALIZE HOW GOOD I AM FOR YOU. THAT ONLY I WILL EVER UNDERSTAND YOU.
SLAM
SNIFF
THERE THERE
YOU WON'T WANT TO HURT MY FEELINGS, AND I WON'T EVER FORCE THE ISSUE. I'LL TELL MYSELF IT'S BECAUSE I "VALUE OUR FRIENDSHIP."

BIT BY BIT, I'LL MAKE YOU DEPEND ON ME.
YOU'LL THINK ABOUT HOW LONG IT WOULD TAKE TO BUILD THIS KIND OF CONNECTION AGAIN.
AND IN A MOMENT OF WEAKNESS
AND LONELINESS
YOU'LL GIVE IN.
IT'LL FEEL COMFORTABLE AND NATURAL. YOU'LL QUIETLY REVISE YOUR DEFINITION OF LOVE AND TRY TO BE HAPPY.
AND SOMETIMES YOU WILL BE.
Friends with detriments.
ONLY THE WISTFULNESS IN YOUR GAZE AND THE TINY PAUSE BEFORE YOU SAY "I LOVE YOU" WILL HINT THAT THIS WASN'T THE ENDING YOU'D HOPED FOR.
SOUND GOOD?
... I'M GOING TO DATE THIS JERK.
BUT HE DOESN'T RESPECT YOU!

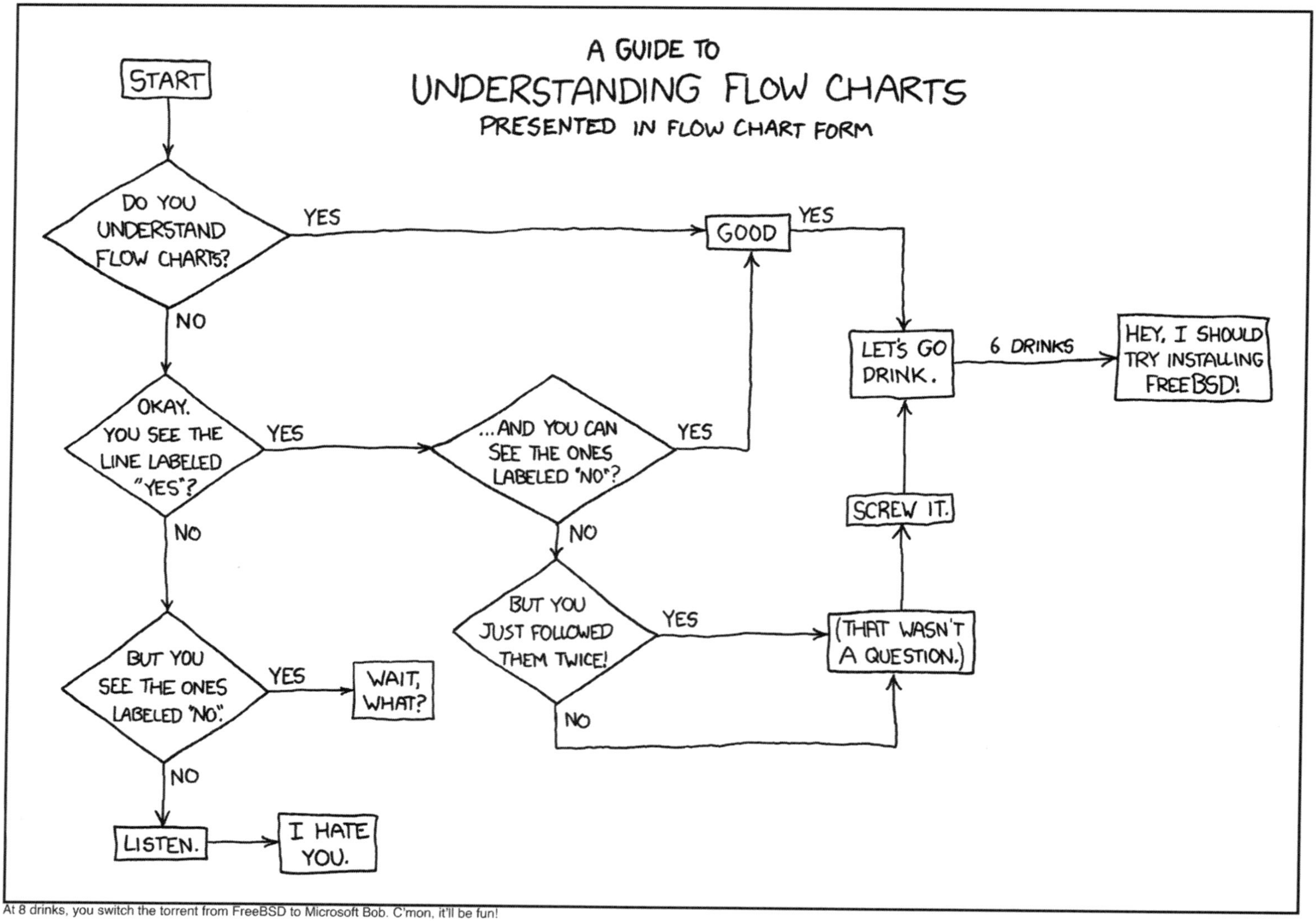
A GUIDE TO
UNDERSTANDING FLOW CHARTS
PRESENTED IN FLOW CHART FORM
START
DO YOU UNDERSTAND FLOW CHARTS?
YES
GOOD
YES
NO
LET'S GO DRINK.
6 DRINKS
HEY, I SHOULD TRY INSTALLING FREEBSD!
OKAY. YOU SEE THE LINE LABELED "YES"?
YES
...AND YOU CAN SEE THE ONES LABELED "NO"?
YES
NO
NO
SCREW IT.
BUT YOU JUST FOLLOWED THEM TWICE!
YES
(THAT WASN'T A QUESTION.)
NO
BUT YOU SEE THE ONES LABELED "NO".
YES
WAIT, WHAT?
NO
LISTEN.
I HATE YOU.

At 8 drinks, you switch the torrent from FreeBSD to Microsoft Bob. C'mon, it'll be fun!

MORE DRINKING

SO HOW FAR DID YOU GET WITH HER?
SECOND BASE?
WAIT, WHICH ONE IS THAT? BELOW THE WAIST, BUT... NOT UNDER THE CLOTHES?
I THINK THAT'S... SHORTSTOP?
YOU SHOULD TRY CROSSING THE PITCHER'S MOUND.
THEN DOWN THE 50-YARD LINE, AND RIGHT PAST HER TEN-PIN.
SOUNDS TRICKY.
YEAH. LAST TIME I TRIED IT, I GOT A RED FLAG.
IF YOU KNOW WHAT I MEAN.
I REALLY DON'T.

I once got to second base with a basketball player. She was so confused.

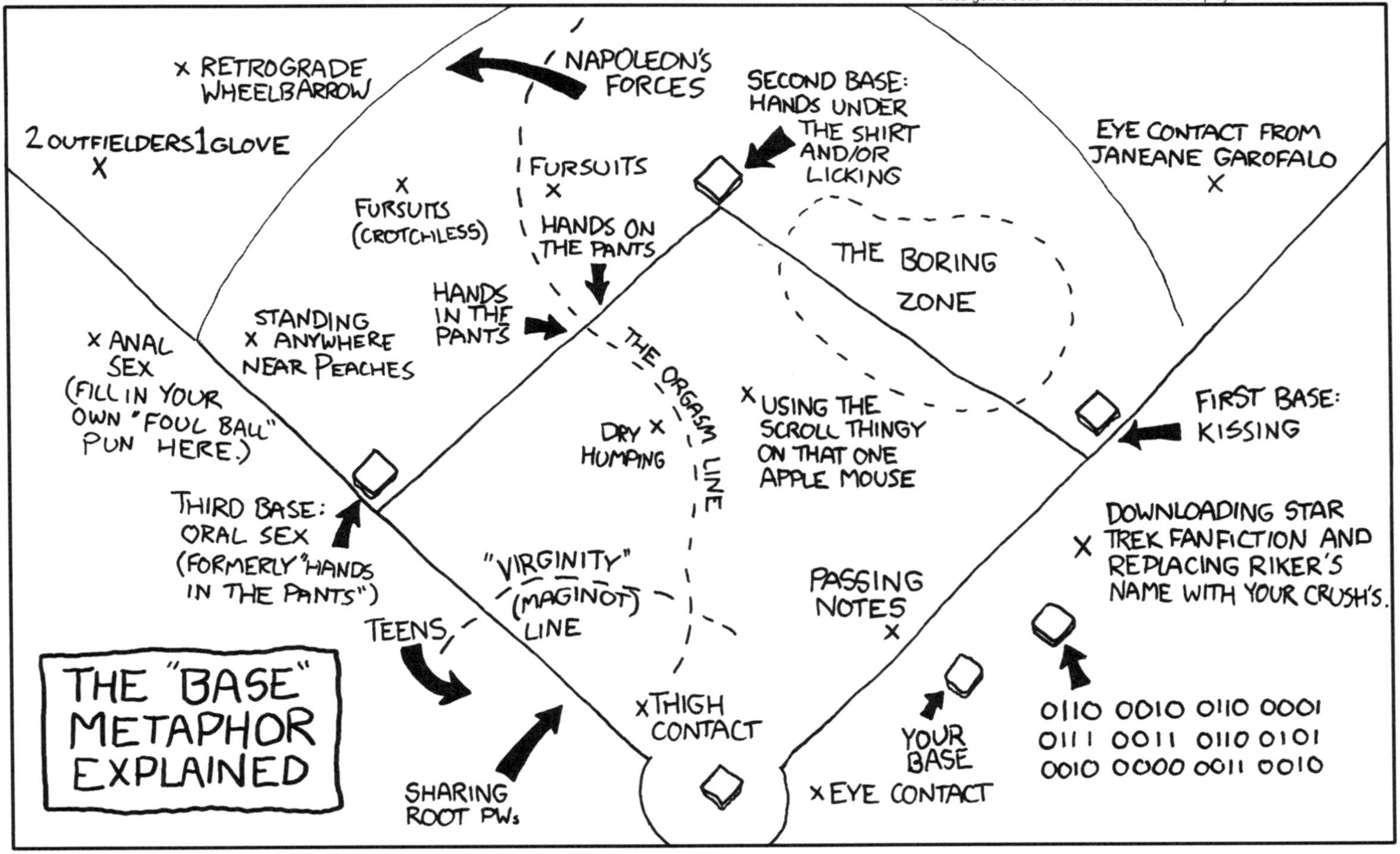
THE "BASE" METAPHOR EXPLAINED
× RETROGRADE WHEELBARROW
NAPOLEON'S FORCES
2 OUTFIELDERS 1 GLOVE ×
× FURSUITS (CROTCHLESS)
FURSUITS ×
HANDS ON THE PANTS
SECOND BASE: HANDS UNDER THE SHIRT AND/OR LICKING
EYE CONTACT FROM JANEANE GAROFALO ×
THE BORING ZONE
HANDS IN THE PANTS
STANDING × ANYWHERE NEAR PEACHES
× ANAL SEX (FILL IN YOUR OWN "FOUL BALL" PUN HERE.)
THE ORGASM LINE
DRY × HUMPING
× USING THE SCROLL THINGY ON THAT ONE APPLE MOUSE
FIRST BASE: KISSING
THIRD BASE: ORAL SEX (FORMERLY "HANDS IN THE PANTS")
"VIRGINITY" (MAGINOT) LINE
DOWNLOADING STAR TREK FANFICTION AND REPLACING RIKER'S NAME WITH YOUR CRUSH'S.
PASSING NOTES ×
TEENS
× THIGH CONTACT
YOUR BASE
0110 0010 0110 0001
0111 0011 0110 0101
0010 0000 0011 0010
SHARING ROOT PWs
× EYE CONTACT

THREE YEARS AGO, THE KINGDOM OF LIATE OVERTHREW THEIR OLD ORDER AND ESTABLISHED A CONSTITUTIONAL MONARCHY. OUR LEADERS SIGNED A TREATY WITH THEIR QUEEN, AND OUR BORDERS WERE SET BY THE YARBIS ACCORDS.
MANY SAID WAR WOULD BE UNENDING, THAT PEACE WOULD ALWAYS BE A DREAM DEFERRED.
BUT TODAY, OUR FLAG FLIES PROUDLY OVER OUR EMBASSY IN THEIR KINGDOM, AND THEY WALK OUR LANDS WITHOUT FEAR.
SO COME, TRAVELER. LAY DOWN YOUR GRUDGES AND JOIN US IN BROTHERHOOD. IT IS TIME NOT TO FIGHT, BUT TO LIVE.
THIS IS THE WORST CAPTURE-THE-FLAG SERVER EVER.

Eventually a UN is set up. And then a lone rebel runs down the line of flags in front of it, runs back to his base, and gets a kajillion points.

-EMAIL ACCOUNT SETUP-
TO VERIFY YOUR IDENTITY, WE NEED TO ASK YOU A QUESTION NOBODY ELSE COULD ANSWER.
Q: WHERE ARE THE BODIES BURIED?
A: BEHIND THE
BEHIND THE ...NICE TRY.
DAMN.

Let's invite him to a party and play 'I never'. Okay, I never hid any bodies SOUTH of Main Street. ... he's taking a drink!

110112

I USED TO THINK CORRELATION IMPLIED CAUSATION.
THEN I TOOK A STATISTICS CLASS. NOW I DON'T.
SOUNDS LIKE THE CLASS HELPED.
WELL, MAYBE.

Correlation doesn't imply causation, but it does waggle its eyebrows sugestively and gesture furtively while mouthing 'look over there'.

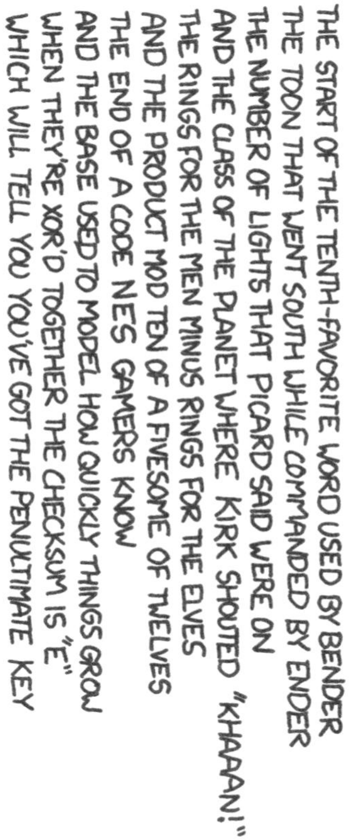
THE START OF THE TENTH-FAVORITE WORD USED BY BENDER
THE TOON THAT WENT SOUTH WHILE COMMANDED BY ENDER
THE NUMBER OF LIGHTS THAT PICARD SAID WERE ON
AND THE CLASS OF THE PLANET WHERE KIRK SHOUTED "KHAAAN!"
THE RINGS FOR THE MEN MINUS RINGS FOR THE ELVES
AND THE PRODUCT MOD TEN OF A FIVESOME OF TWELVES
THE END OF A CODE NES GAMERS KNOW
AND THE BASE USED TO MODEL HOW QUICKLY THINGS GROW
WHEN THEY'RE XOR'D TOGETHER THE CHECKSUM IS "E"
WHICH WILL TELL YOU YOU'VE GOT THE PENULTIMATE KEY

MY HOBBY:
APPENDING "NO PUN INTENDED" TO LINES WITH NO PUN IN THEM.
I THINK HE'S INTERNALIZED HIS GIRLFRIEND'S ATTITUDES— NO PUN INTENDED—AND SO...
THREE HOURS LATER:
"INTERNALIZED"? LIED? ANALYZED? OR IS IT "ATTITUDES"? DAMMIT.

Like spelling 'dammit' correctly -- with two m's -- it's a troll that works best on the most literate.

110120

HEY, LET'S TROLL THE FUCK OUT OF THE TWILIGHT BOARDS
I'M IN
SHOULD BE FUN
ME TOO.
SIGNING ON NOW.
LOL ANGSTY TEENS.
HOURS LATER:
HI, IT'S STEPHENIE MEYER. FINE, YOU DON'T LIKE MY BOOKS, BUT PLEASE LEAVE US ALONE.
SHOW US YOUR TITS.
I ASKED POLITELY. DON'T MAKE ME GET TOUGH.
AND WHAT, CALL THE INTERNET POLICE? YOU DON'T GET IT, DO YOU? WE'VE BEEN TROLLING FOR YEARS. WE'RE ALL ANONYMOUS. THERE'S NOTHING YOU CAN DO TO HURT US. WE'RE THE NET'S HATE MACHINE.
OKAY. JUST REMEMBER, I GAVE YOU A CHANCE.
DISCONNECTED
SIX MONTHS LATER:
VAMPIRES! BOOK VI
EDWARD RAN A PALE HAN
THROUGH HIS PERFECT GOLDEN-
BRONZE HAIR, THEN SIGNED
ON TO 4CHAN.ORG, THE DARKEST
PLACE ON THE INTERNET, WHERE
ALL HIS VAMPIRE COMPATRIOTS
SPENT THEIR TIME.
SUDDENLY, THERE WAS
KNOCK AT THE D
SWEPT IN.
SHORTLY THEREAFTER:
OMG I LOVE THIS PLACE ITS SO EDGY BEING ANONYMOUS
DAWN!
WHOS YOUR FAVORITE VAMPIRE
CHECK OUT MY PIC IM SO DARK JUST LIKE THIS SITE
ANY TWILIGHT FANS IN DALLAS WANT TO MEET A LONELY
OH... OH GOD.
We have met the enemy and he is us.

110200

SOME 4CHANNERS WROTE IN TO COMPLAIN THAT I WAS BREAKING RULES 1 AND 2. SOME 4CHANNERS ARE A LITTLE SLOW ON THE UPTAKE.

1... 2...
BAAA
...1,306... 1,307...
BAAA
...32,767...-32,768...
BAAA BAAAA
BAAA
?
...-32,767...-32,766...
BAAA

If androids someday DO dream of electric sheep, don't forget to declare sheepCount as a long int.

MAN, SEX HAS ALL THESE CRAZY SOCIAL RULES. THEY JUST CREATE DRAMA.
LET'S AGREE TO CHANGE THEM, AND MAKE SEX SIMPLE!
OKAY!
HOORAY! WE'VE SOLVED THE PROBLEM OF DRAMA!
I'LL GO TELL EVERYONE!
DRAMA
TIME
RULE CHANGE
HOLY SHIT
GUYS
PEOPLE ARE COMPLICATED!

This happens in geek circles every so often. The 'Hey, this is just a system I can figure out easily!' is also a problem among engineers first diving into the stock market.

123 B

VRDSYLRBYSMRLUVRXGCFHZWXKYNHYKLKWMCLRMFIKOZAIYXJWITOYOVN

111000

THE TRACKING TAG WILL RECORD THE SHARK'S MOVEMENT AND HABITS.
THEN, IT WILL POP FREE AND FLOAT TO THE SURFACE.
WE CAN'T AFFORD A RECOVERY PROGRAM, SO THE CAPSULES WILL INFLATE HELIUM BALLOONS, DRIFT OVER LAND,
AND HOPEFULLY BE FOUND AND MAILED TO US. ANY QUESTIONS?
IF FOUND PLEASE CALL
CHUNK
SPLOOSH
!!!
CLICK
HISSSS
??
AAAAAAAA
CHOMP CHOMP
DADDY?
YES?
I WANT TO BE A SCIENTIST.

Completely implausible? Yes. Nevertheless, worth keeping a can of shark repellent next to the bed.